Last Orders
at the
Changamire Arms

Robin Walker

PILLAR

INTERNATIONAL PUBLISHING

Published by Pillar International Publishing Ltd.

www.IndiePillar.com

Cover Design by Zoodle Design

ISBN-13: 978-0-9574598-1-6

DEDICATION

With eternal gratitude to my wife, Sandra, whose industry enabled me to get on with the easy stuff - write the damn thing.

And to all the good men and women of Rhodesia whose only sin was to trust the devious people who run the world.

And finally, to Mark Lloyd, who held my hand through the minefields of editing.

Introduction

In March 1965, I took a step that would change the course of my life. I left Birmingham, England (not Alabama) and emigrated with my young wife and family to Rhodesia. I spent the next eight years teaching but, though the schools were very good, the standard of education very high and the pupils, both black and white, were a pleasure to teach, the job was poorly paid and I had a small family to support. It was time, therefore, to move on.

We had decided within a couple of years of our arrival that we wanted to spend our lives in Rhodesia - good, honest people, wide open spaces, fresh air, sunshine the year round and a good education for the children.

All the myths we had been bombarded with before we left England had been dispelled - that, for instance, African domestic staff were treated like slaves, when in fact they were treated with kindness and generosity, that Rhodesians would not allow Africans access to public places such as buses, trains, bars and the rest, because the world always confused South Africa with its apartheid system and Rhodesia that had no such thing.

We had even begun using first person plurals instead of third person plurals in our letters to England. Rhodesians were no longer 'they' but 'we'.

'No, Aunt Jane. We do not make our African servants wear ankle-irons.' Or:

'No, Bill. We don't put them in stocks for bad behaviour.'

We had ceased calling England 'back home' - an old colonial expression that was an insult to the native population (Rhodesians were never ex-patriates). England had become 'in U.K.' or 'in Britain', expressions used by people who, like us, had no intention of ever going 'back home' to live. Most criticisms of Rhodesia, we found, were made by people who wouldn't have been able to find the country on a map. And it mystified me how much people knew about Rhodesia, its life and politics, when they couldn't recite their tables beyond five times six equals eleven, or who didn't know why the marathon race was called 'the marathon.'

4

What they never seemed to know, however, was that Rhodesia fed the whole of Central Africa, even during the terrorist war: that they fought in both world wars, that Rhodesian pilots had fought and died in the Battle of Britain; that to this day Rhodesians were not allowed to take part in Remembrance Day Parades; that when they fled from Mugabe's Zimbabwe they left behind for him to play with and ruin one of the strongest economies in the world. So much for sanctions.

Enoch Powell summed it up when he was heard to say on Rhodesian television:

'This is my second visit to Rhodesia: so you might say I'm now an expert on the country's affairs.' Satire at its best.

Rhodesians were mostly of British stock, going back generations or recently arrived in the country, so that if a visitor to Rhodesia, a journalist, say, chose to call me a racist I would reply, absentmindedly tapping a sjambok against my right boot,

'Of course I am. It's the British blood, don't yer know.'

So I left teaching and joined the Ministry of Internal Affairs (see Glossary) where there awaited work that was as varied and complex as it was fascinating, where we would both come upon a side of Africa we hadn't even suspected existed and, best of all, where we would meet, carouse and work with the most remarkable people this earth of ours has to offer, some of whom you yourself will meet in the following pages.

Glossary

S.I.A. - Secretary for Internal Affairs

P.C. - Provincial Commissioner

D.C. - District Commissioner

A.D.C. - Assistant District Commissioner

S.D.O. - Senior District officer

D.O. - District Officer

A.O. - Agricultural Officer

P.D.O. - Primary Development Officer

F.A. - Field Assistant

I.A.N.S. - Internal Affairs National Serviceman

Vedettes - Civilians, doing 6-week call-ups

D.A. - District Assistant

D.S.A. - District Security Assistant

A.D.F - African Development Fund. A fund used exclusively for the development of tribal land.

Changamire Arms - The Intaf pub, pronounced Changa-<u>mee</u>-ree

Ops Room. - Operations Room

P.V. - Protected Village

R.L.I. - Rhodesian Light Infantry

J.O.C. - Joint Operations Committee

O.C. - Officer Commanding

P.S.O. - Protected Sub-Office

Casevac - Casualty Evacuation

S.B. - Special Branch (Police)

Pronto - Radio Operator (Army)

T.F. - Territorial Forces (Army)

ters - terrorists

Browns - General term for Army

Blues - Ditto for Air Force

Notes on Internal Affairs

The Ministry of Internal Affairs was mainly concerned with two things: civil administration, which was a clerical thing-keeping records of births and deaths, collecting taxes, organising elections, and so on; and, in tribal areas to establish and maintain infrastructure - roads and bridges, schools and clinics, hospitals and water supplies, and the many other forms of infrastructure that people in the west take for granted.

In order to qualify as a D.C., people (men and women) had to pass certain exams which gave them points, there being eight points in all. These were: law exams worth 4 points, Customs and Administration exams worth 2 points, and African language exams, written and oral, worth 2 points. In addition to these qualifications one would need a number of years' experience in every aspect of the work involved, and would have to be deemed proficient in every facet. This was determined by annual reports and eventually a promotions board interview.

One could not become an A.D.C. without all eight points, a S.D.O. would probably have four to six points and a great deal of experience, while a D.O. would have four points and adequate experience at lower levels.

The exams were tough and provided a stumbling block to promotion for many aspirants who might well spend their entire careers as S.D.O.s or D.O.s if that was what made them happy.

Many young cadets joining the ministry did so because they were lured by the possibility of a little bush life, including minimal licensed hunting and occasional weekends fishing.

When the war came, however, they were unable to move freely about the tribal areas and had to learn, through training, how to cope with the dangers by which they were surrounded in order to fulfil their duties as administrators.

Robin Walker

CHAPTER 1

JOCK

An early casualty of changing philosophies, alas, The Windsor Hotel, a weary, early twentieth-century, Salisbury relic grimly hanging on like the whites who used her, was a victim of her own obsolescent style, at odds with a new world she did not understand. She tried yielding to demands for fashionable cocktail bars and grillrooms but she was just no good. Cosmetic surgery was not enough for, behind the condescending façade, original rooms still lingered on, sinful, inflexible, and wilfully unadaptable. It was total, radical change or go. The Windsor went. She gave up her site to polystyrene shops that would soon overflow with cheap foreign muck and worthless local trash, and went.

She was a game enough bird though, in her time. I once passed a night in one of her dilapidated, feather-bare wings and when I got to my room and turned on what management called the light I found myself surrounded by furniture that gave me austere looks and frowned at my dress – a great disdainful solid oak wardrobe, a dressing table of solid beechwood, its mirror yellow and fly-blown, and designed for women of a more robust era, a brass bedstead with a feather mattress you knew would yield to no nonsense.

Down a bleak, dungeon-dark corridor – Rhodes' ghost leapt out and shouted 'Diamonds' at me if I whistled – the bathroom lay like a malevolent spirit patiently in wait. And in it the bath. I remember cast-iron feet, splayed to bear the weight, and twin brass taps which, ever dripping like a child's nostrils, had scored parallel blue-green ski-trails down its white enamel slope.

The only available water was cold, a fact I mentioned once to one David, a friend, who always stayed at The Windsor when in town, but he had spent many years in India with the British Army and doubtless knew about these things. 'Of course there's no bloody hot water,' says he, his scarlet cheeks deepening to purple. 'There never is. Not in places like The Windsor.' My curiosity sagged beneath the weight of his blustering hotelmanship and I went elsewhere. He grew tobacco when he wasn't in some pub.

Breakfast was served downstairs in the Blue Room, everything blue including the language when the waiters were hung over – surly black looks if you wanted two eggs. The Red Room was the newly-appointed (using brochure language) cocktail bar which, as the war dragged on, became a refuge for wealthy, nerve-shot, alcoholic farmers and their carefully-spoken, dilapidated wives. There was also the iniquitous Long Bar, a swillers' paradise, and 'twas thus thither that Jock and I now made our slovenly way.

You could not, even had you created him, call Jock a man of letters. He was the product of an age that had long since sacrificed beauty on the altar of expediency and had no need of letters. For the pen is subservient to the sword in a world that is governed by ignorance. No. Jock had been a Royal Marine aboard the Fearless, a sword and gourd affair if ever there was, that time Wilson, the sophisticated envoy of Perfidious Albion, and Smith, the fresh Rhodesian Front whipping boy with a war-hero image (shot down by an irate Italian spaghetti farmer) had discovered a number of things in common, not least British ancestry, but they had made their promises, as politicians will, and this barred their way to compromise. Wilson still had weeks in mind while the slower Smith, having something to lose, required a thousand years: the time he believed African democracy needed to ripen. Some thought a thousand insufficient, such is cynicism.

By the mid-seventies Jock was R.S.M. of the Rhodesian Light Infantry, and I had come to know him in Mt. Darwin where I was A.D.C. with the Ministry of Internal Affairs. This meant that my immediate boss was the D.C. which meant I was general dogsbody which meant I was in the crap whenever things went wrong which meant every two minutes. However ….

I was on a rare shopping trip to Salisbury and was crossing a main road, my shopping done, when a polite but determined Glaswegian voice elbowed its way through the mid-morning racket and fell upon my ears. Jock. I knew suddenly the dread Scotland's ancient enemies came to know when the wind carried down to them the hideous warning notes of bagpipes being warmed up for action.

A hot shower of apprehension ran down the back of my neck and I hastened on, feigning deafness.

'How are you?' he says, now beside me, one hand resting on my arm.

I stopped. 'I've got shopping to do,' I said, lying hotly.

'Aye. But we've time for a couple.' He was a beer-gutted, red-faced, sandy-haired little bastard with a fierce, unquenchable appetite for punch-ups. He could barely have reached my chin in a brawl but he could reach my baubles twain and the knowledge made me feel naked. I regarded him as a friend but one had to box clever, never being sure, and I held his powers of destruction in greater awe than I did the traffic that swirled about us.

'Just a couple then,' says some yellow-belly inside me, and we headed for where we came in.

The Long Bar was packed with members of the armed forces and knowing Jock as I did I made a mental note of all the exits and their 'pozzies' as we devil-may-cares knew them. I shoved the shopping inside the bar-rail and awaited developments. When we came to our second brandies my little bundle of northern dissipation says to me -

'Tell you what.'

When someone says 'Tell you what' as a preamble to a bright idea I usually answer, with enough enthusiasm to generate indifference, 'What?' and carry on wondering if the barmaid's boobs are real or contrived, but when Jock used it, it meant the devil had hi-jacked his mind and was about to use it to embroil others, me included, in the infliction of pain and the destruction of the immediate environment.

'What?' Me, a-quiver.

'You start that end I'll start this.'

I knew what he intended. A quick brawl before lunch. A primordial hors d'oeuvre harking back to the cave when primitive man had to fight his neighbour for hunting rights.

'Right,' says I, like one unable to wait.

Downing my drink I walked smartly to the far end of the bar, burst through the double doors, made my way through steaming kitchens, past toilets, down an alley lined with empty beer crates and into the welcoming bosom of the waiting traffic.

'Damn,' I thought as I crossed the road. But I wasn't going back.

I haven't seen Jock since then, but the grapevine informed me shortly after that he'd taken a drop of leave in the U.K. His wife ran a fish and chip shop on some beach-front and Jock, not being expected home, found her lolling in bed with a fellow who, I was told, when Jock had finished expressing his disappointment in the only way he knew how, was scarce distinguishable from the battered cod his wife purveyed for a living.

Jock could, I suppose, have sent him a nice letter suggesting he have some consideration for the feelings of others, but, as I say, I don't think Jock could write.

CHAPTER 2

GEORDIE AND FRIENDS

Geordie was our mechanic, call-sign 'Bluebell'. And a bloody fine Bluebell was he. It was difficult in those days to get good men for the workshops, there being a war on and all, and the ones we did employ were either strangers to basic mechanical principles, bone idle, drunks, or a sorry combination of all three. I had hired and fired so many of these itinerant misfits that when Bill, a member of our field staff, told me that a friend of his, a mechanic, was looking for work I didn't make a dash for the office and do cartwheels.

Bill was an Irishman, more often than not a violent one, and though great at his job he sometimes needed direction – a good ballocking, that is. I had no illusions about any of Bill's friends.

Now field staff in a war zone were, erm, how do I put this? Clichés are mildly helpful – rough diamonds, good as gold, salt of the earth – but they don't somehow do the subjects justice. Perhaps they will emerge of themselves as the narrative meanders along and gathers drift-wood as it goes. Drift-wood? I suppose they were in a way. By trade they were carpenters, builders, painters, but when they turned their grimy hands to Internal Affairs (Intaf) work they had to be jacks of every trade. Pubs got most of their pay.

Not therefore expecting much, I called Bill's friend in for an interview. Even wore a jacket and tie for the occasion. What came through my office door was a shortish, big-bellied, ill-shaven, waddling heap of filth that was short on shirt and trouser buttons and wouldn't have been out of place in a dustbin. Its name was Geordie. It helped itself to a chair, put its fag out in the flowerpot, coughed and broke wind. I don't know why, when so much else about him clamoured like greedy fledglings for attention, but I found myself transfixed by the sorry plight of his finger-nails, ugly, broken, tobacco-stained remnants that they were. Perhaps they symbolised the man. He didn't inspire much confidence, strangely enough, and I didn't give much for his chances.

After a couple of minutes I thanked him for coming and escorted him to the door.

'You haven't,' says he in his broad Geordie accent, 'asked me about me drinking habits.'

'Should I?'

'I always get asked about me drinking habits.'

Something inside began to wriggle. Was there more to him? I heard myself asking for his references and he produced a wad of dirt that looked like a rat's nest. I shook out the dust, the bits of tobacco and pocket fluff, and noticed, like a palaeontologist with a badly preserved manuscript, words written there closely resembling our 'reliable', 'capable' and 'loyal'. Though my instincts cried out in anguish when they learnt what I was about to do, I took him on. And we never looked back.

We had something like fifty assorted vehicles - diesel, petrol - and Geordie kept them on their feet almost single-handed. He had no education to talk of, owing to an attack of polio which kept him in hospital for three years during his early teens. He will tell you how during his incarceration his aunt, who was responsible for him, would make her way to his bedside each day, there to fidget for half an hour while her mind travelled across continents in search of something to say. Geordie would lie helplessly, like a beached squid, and pray for her to go.

At the age of fifteen he left hospital and went almost immediately into an apprenticeship, learning thus that prayers don't always go unanswered, and emerged seven years later with the highest qualifications in the land. He was blessed with humility, doubtless born of pain and despair, and took pills daily to keep himself alive, each day being a lovely, blessed thing.

He never complained.

When he met someone for the first time, be it the Prime Minister or a tramp in a pub, he would hold himself loftily aloof without losing that air of disarming deference and casual courtliness: light up a fag, break wind, scratch his arse and waddle away. If we had a posh do with V.I.P.s in attendance we offered up quiet prayers that

Geordie would keep away. For though we were fond of the little beggar and would die rather than cause him hurt, unlike Geordie we had illusions and feared his ways would be mistaken for the norm. Not that we needed fear. Geordie was at peace with himself and the world about him and would only pitch up when invited. We could keep all the social embroidery; Geordie was his own man.

One Christmas my wife, Sandra, and I joined Geordie and a couple of his friends for lunch. The only thing he possessed was a rickety old suitcase held together with a length of string, and in it a hammock, spare shirt and trousers. 'Cos you can sleep any bloody where if you gotta hammock.' The house in which he lived, moved and had his being belonged to Intaf and was equipped with essentials only – heavy furniture comprising bed, dining-room table and chairs, cooker and fridge.

He had bought a turkey you could just get through the door and made arrangements with the Q.M. of the R.L.I. to have it cooked in their ovens. I don't know what arrangements they were but a clapped-out old Land Rover belonging to Intaf went missing around this time and for all our investigations we never discovered what happened to it.

Anyway, the turkey. We had been sitting around making small talk and drinking best South African wine out of used baked-bean tins when Geordie says, 'Right. Who's hungry?' and disappeared into the kitchen.

We only expected baked beans and sausage and suchlike and were filled with contrition when he reappeared moments later scarce visible beneath a mountain of steaming flesh. He laid the beast down on the table with all appropriate ceremony (lies: he flung it down with a mighty crash), disappeared once more into the kitchen and returned shortly laden with plates he might well have bought in a jumble sale. Whatever one's taste in porcelain, be it colour, shape, size or pattern, Geordie had catered for it. Ditto knives and forks. Nothing matched – even baked bean alias wine tins were shamelessly grouped together with erstwhile pilchard, peaches, and peas. Gravy in an old oil can. And he had unique way with him at the table.

'Who wants a drumstick?' which is promptly wrestled from the creature's breast and hurled across the table at you. It is then up to you to bring off an athletic slip-catch before it hits the floor. The carcass he hacks up with an obscure implement he's nicked from the local garage and thrusts it by the handful – handful – onto your plate. Peas he empties from a tin and potatoes you pluck out of the air.

'Help yourselves to gravy,' he says through a mouthful and we all dig in.

'Where,' asks Derek, one of the guests, 'did you acquire your remarkable table manners?'

'Hospital,' says Geordie, belching, breaking wind.

'So, Yarra,' says I when the lunch things had been cleared away – Derek suggested chucking them away but Geordie said, no, he had a dinner party early in the New Year – 'when are you going on this trip to the Seychelles?'

Yarrawonga, an outcast from the Australian outback, I had taken on because Bill Irish had recommended him. I discovered in the passing of time that Bill, Geordie and Yarra had been drinking pals for years. Indeed I once asked Bill where he had met Yarra, a rhetorical question really - library? art gallery? - but I got -

'Where the bloody hell d'yer think?'

Yarra's responsibilities – a word he wouldn't have understood – involved the construction of roads, bridges, lavatories, brothels, pubs – not pubs, sorry, it just slipped out – and it took him to some distinctly inhospitable parts of the bush. The bush was never asked its opinion. It took what it was given.

Australians, you see - well those at least that stumbled into my path - are nothing more than cellular, protoplasmic if you like, disaster areas. They ricochet witlessly from crisis to crisis, curiously unaware of the mayhem and devastation that constitutes their wake, and to follow them around as they go about their daily business is much like walking in the aftermath of a tornado. Yet they themselves survive. And Yarra, though an unassuming sample of his native breed, quiet, almost shy you might say, was nevertheless Australian. You could tell by his wake. You always knew where he'd been. He ricocheted.

He came from a small town in Australia called Yarrawonga (really) which I am told is somewhere near a stretch of the River

Murray. This doubtless explains why, if you wanted to rile him, rouse him from his placid, almost moribund state of being, all you needed do was remark, preferably with a cool and knowing authority,

'There are of course no fish in the Murray.'

Yarra, as I have indicated, was a sleepy, well-nigh dormant, sort of creature for all his Aussie blood and could fall asleep anywhere, time or how. He might, for instance, fall quietly asleep at the end of the bar, his head drooping forward contentedly and coming to rest on the top of the beer bottle, but only let someone say, be it quiet as snowflakes falling -

'There's no fish of course, not in the Murray.'

and Yarra would jerk awake, his hands instinctively curling themselves into fists and coming up into the punching position. You now gauge the distance between you and Yarra and prepare for exit.

'Whadyar mean,' he'd say. 'Who says? Let me tell you lot right here and now. I've caught fish in the Murray that big,' and he stretches his arms out in the classic fisherman's fib position. Geordie just couldn't resist it. We would all be talking about rugby, cricket, the clandestine habits of waffles, whatever, and Geordie would suddenly pipe up,

'There are, of course, no fish in the Murray.'

and Yarra would surface from his reveries, ready to punch the nearest face he could reach.

In all other respects Yarra was content with the ways of the world and the demands of his fellow man and could handle catastrophes, disasters, holocausts, without changing gear. Where you and I would be heading for the funny farm, Yarra would merely lean back his head, open his crumbling, brown face, home of crumbling, brown teeth, and rattle the cocktail glasses with guileless Aussie larfter. Which is good. Because things, diabolical things, things that didn't care about the consequences of their actions, never ceased to happen to him. You could blow him up in a landmine, ambush him, pinch his girlfriend, hide his beer while he went for a wee, and Yarra would simply subside like detonated snow beneath cavernous, brown larfter, put his feet up on the bar and go to sleep. But – I still duck instinctively, 'There's no fish in the Murray.' and you got a mean-tempered,

'Whadyar mean? Who says? Let me tell you lot ....' He was like one of his fish, went for it every time. Geordie just couldn't resist it.

We lost him in the end. He and Geordie went for a month's leave, on that trip to the Seychelles, and when Geordie reappeared, shagged out, two months later, he told us how Yarra had become unpopular with certain authorities, run out of money and excuses, surrendered his passport, and returned to his native Australia.

The very last I heard of him was that he'd been drummed out of his home town for doing something socially unacceptable (Socially unacceptable. That's like saying you killed one of your pigs for rolling in the mud.) and was headed back for Rhodesia. But we never saw him again.

I often wonder though if there really are any fish in the Murray. I must ask Yarra next time I see him. He's bound to know.

CHAPTER 3

DEREK

Geordie's friendship with Derek, a large block of a man with a dry, throwaway sense of humour, I can only put down to the attraction of opposites, because, though they were both gentlemen, they were the products of systems that were unbridgeably poles apart, Geordie being of lowly if proud origins and Derek the outcome of an English Public School education, a commission with the British Army, and an altercation or two on the battlefield with some of Hitler's troops. I cannot recall Geordie ever lighting a woman's cigarette or standing up when she entered the room, nor Derek breaking wind and scratching his arse. But there you are. Friendships passeth all understanding.

The office block was a confusing honeycomb of offices, a beehive of activity that, to be generous for a moment, we'll classify as work. In this busy little hive, however, there were drones and one of them, not wishing to stretch the generosity bit too far, was Derek. The desk he occupied belonged to the Ministry of Lands, he being a Lands Inspector who would normally be expected to visit farms in the area and advise against erosion and other evils of uneducated practice.

And in a perfect world he might have been out there all the hours that God sent encouraging local farmers to dig contours. Contour ridges, for those who like to know things, serve as a kind of basic, very basic, form of terracing, which creates a micro-catchment area for rows of crops. In years of scanty rainfall, it steers every drop of water to where it does most good, and in over-generous years it prevents all the topsoil from washing away into the rivers. This splendid agricultural practice, you understand, was not taken up spontaneously by local farmers - digging contours was hard work, and more so when the digger was not convinced of the necessity for digging them in the first place. So the Lands Inspector jollied them along, surveying their lands and marking out with pegs the areas that were to be dug. And paid follow-up visits later when he might not be quite so jolly if things hadn't progressed.

Derek's problem was boredom. He was rarely able to get out and do inspections, there being so many other demands on armed escorts into the field, and I have known him stamp out of his office in rage and frustration, and risk his life without an escort in order to have a drink with a friend.

The first time I saw him he caused me some confusion, because he seemed not know where he was or what he was doing. Into one office, out of another, stumble into a wall, and as he was new I assumed he was simply having trouble finding his way around. But the following morning the same. Up the stairs, zig-zag down the corridor, disappear. Was he? He couldn't be. He was. Well, not drunk exactly, nor exactly sober.

I have seen him in the Intaf pub at 10 o'clock at night when he's been at the brandy all day somewhere and you got no inkling from his demeanour that he'd been at it until his glass eye fell into someone's drink and gave him away. His glass eye was a replacement for the one he had lost to an anti-personnel mine during World War II. He drank two bottles a day and concerned himself with neither time, date nor place, ablative case.

I have mentioned his humour. Unable to find him one day, and needing to speak urgently, I decided to try the caravan where he lived. He was sitting under a great mahogany tree drinking morning tea.

'Aren't you supposed to be at work?' I asked, mildly amused by the hyper-colonial setting.

'Yes,' came the reply in that public school, army officer, drawl, 'but this is far more amusing.'

Or again.

Down to the pub early one morning to take stock, only to find Derek taking his ease in the deep recesses of an armchair and having what is unmistakably a snifter.

'Bit early for that, Derek,' says I. Back it came,

'Well, gin is a morning drink you know.'

He rarely smiled, a symptom of the boredom and irritation from which he suffered, but he would chuckle merrily when someone who had fallen foul of him did the same thing with authority.

'And not before time,' he would say smugly.

One day however his own head office in Salisbury decided to get out the microscope and make a closer study of the little world he sculled around in, and when he was confronted with their findings he was consumed with righteous indignation and spoke to no-one for a week. It went like this. Derek was able to do so little field work he had the best part of a month in which to compile his monthly progress reports, a chore he performed, having a helpful imagination, a facility with words and time to burn, at a cakewalk. Top copies of his reports went to his boss in Salisbury.

He was sitting in his office one day, teaching geckos to do handstands, when in, and utterly out of the blue, dropped aforementioned brass. In Derek's previous report he claimed he had pegged a large farm, a tricky undertaking as much of the land was hilly and difficult. Nevertheless he had persevered, worked like the little soldier he was, and pegged the farm from end to end. He'd reported that the farmer, over-brimming with gratitude ('Well, Rob, it makes them happy to think the people are grateful for all our assistance.'), had rounded up his family, got stuck in and dug all the contours. And it was this success that the head office brass was demanding to see.

Matters didn't get off to a good start because, one, Derek couldn't find the farm in question, and two, when eventually they did get there with a little local assistance, there wasn't a hint, ne'er a trace, scarce a sniff, of a contour to be found. None of which was surprising of course because Derek had never been there.

The scene on their return to Derek's office – comments were made regarding misuse of tax-payers' money, abuse of trust, bone bloody idleness, oh, the complete works on 'Clap-Trap: A Guide for Fence-Sitting Officialdom' – he described to me later with barely controlled fury. If that was how they treated a gentleman of his breeding, says he, thumping the desk, he, who had pissed on the likes of them in the army, would damn well show them. The ballocking had been thoroughly deserved, I think, a fact that managed to avoid Derek's normally ever-watchful intelligence.

He did however show them.

Officials on government business away from home could claim an allowance known as 'S and T' – Subsistence and Traveling.

If, for instance, a D.O. spent a day in the bush he would claim forty cents for the first four hours he spent out there, eighty cents for eight hours, $1.20 for twelve hours. A night spent in the bush entitled him to something mind-shattering like $1.75. A D.O. who spent months by himself in a P.S.O. could claim a whole $49.00 per month. He lived behind baking earthen walls a life of dust, discomfort and desolation, often with no running water, no roof, and no means of escape. He got himself blown up, shot at, and shat on, and received in compensation $49.00, his life having been valued by niggardly bureaucratic governmental scum I wouldn't have allowed near my pigs at roughly ten cents an hour. Hell, scum is too good a word. These bureaucrats sat on their fat backsides behind desks in Salisbury, pulling in exaggerated salaries, while people who worked in the bush risked their lives on a daily basis trying in their small way to keep their country safe to live and work in. You can imagine how badly young people in the cities wanted to join the Ministry. They formed themselves into queues and slept on the pavements, as they do at Wimbledon, merely to obtain an application form.

That anyway was Sub-ha-ha-sistence.

Where was I? Oh yes.

'Traveling' was like when you sort of had a Land Rover. If in Darwin, for instance, you could acquire a Land Rover with bulletproof windows, armour-plating and roll bars – mine protection that is – you could use the vehicle on duty and claim so much per kilometre as traveling expenses.

Derek had one such vehicle. Each month he submitted a claim stating dates, distances traveled, destinations, mileometer readings, times out and in. 'Mileometer" is strictly speaking an odometer but we called them mileometers because they measured distances in kilometres. At the bottom of these hell-inspired forms he would add up all the figures giving himself a month's total kilometres traveled at so much per kilometre and a figure in dollars. Still with me? These then went to head office in Salisbury where they were checked and certified correct, in Derek's case by the official who had ballocked him.

So when Derek put in a claim the month following his showdown for triple his usual amount his boss doubtless did somersaults of untrammeled bliss. Derek was getting out and about, pegging Zambia into the bargain I shouldn't wonder. The ticking off had worked. And like the good little bureaucrat he was, the twerp duly certified the claim correct, signed it, date-stamped it, called his secretary in to post the top copy to Darwin for payment, handed her the two bottom copies to be filed in her office under 'S&T Mount Darwin'.

It now being lunch-time there was nothing more he could, needed or wanted to do, so off he went to the pub round the corner where he met his like-minded bureaucrats whose daily moan was centred round the incompetence of those in the field.

Went back to his office. Oh, and he had the usual meeting in the afternoon until the office closed, so the other form that had to be signed, certified and date-stamped would now have to wait until the morrow when he'd be fresh and in the right spirits.

How the country would have survived so long without them, well, I for one will never fathom. It's certainly what's wrong with the world today. Not enough bureaucrats. Take the EU, for instance. But I digress.

The months went by, the claims getting higher and higher and suddenly, one month, too high.

Out he comes. Admires Derek's Land Rover while really noting the mileage on his clock (the Land Rover's, that is), goes suspiciously back to Salisbury. Checks previous claim forms on Derek's file, finds readings more or less correct. Awaits next claim. Claim comes in. Date and mileage smack on.

But he isn't quite satisfied. He now does something Derek, clever little piss-cat, has already done. Taking a piece of string, he lays it along the winding routes Derek's claim forms claim he has traveled on a map.

All distances correct. His man in Darwin is telling the truth. He really is visiting all these out-of-the-way places. You see. All these fellows in the bush need is a little fatherly guidance and, hey presto, they're out there getting stuck in and working their little botty-poohs off.

Ah yes. Many's the hour I've spent under that lovely mahogany tree, contentedly taking tea with Derek, while his Land Rover purred away in the background, its back-axle propped up on blocks of wood, the wheels churning out the mileage.

CHAPTER 4

VEDETTES

I was sitting, early one Monday morning, in the upstairs loo when I heard a dull thud. The water in the lavatory pan, I noticed, had suddenly become subject to a tiny tidal system - backwards, forwards - which threw up inquisitive little fingers of spray against my exposed lower buttocks.

The office block was a grey, two-storey affair and housed all departments of the civil service, though most offices were occupied by Internal Affairs (Intaf). The armoury was situated in the basement and it was from there, I knew, that the noise had emanated. So I finished what I was doing with hurried little movements and rushed downstairs. I expected the worst as had become my wont, having learnt that only thus did one develop a defence stubborn enough to survive the occasional pleasant surprise.

Because of certain, possibly fatal, consequences the accidental discharge (A.D.) had come to be regarded by those with nothing better to occupy their minds than the safety of others (they were nervous wrecks after a month in Darwin) as a serious breach of discipline. So as we lacked the benefits of a disciplinary code and hadn't at that time fiddled government funds to build detention barracks, I took orders twice a week and dispensed what we all knew to be justice in its most unpretentious form. The penalty for an A.D. if you were white was a month's salary and a smack round the ear. A black man on the other hand got a month's salary and a smack round the ear. And that was about as just as it got.

I wasn't surprised on entering the armoury to find one man lying on the floor and one man standing up. Now different people react differently to A.D.s. The guy receiving the bullet falls to the ground but you need fear nothing from him. The one standing up, however, is another kettle of fish and sometimes does strange things. He may become hysterical which makes him dangerous because he won't think to clear the weapon and by the time you arrive he could be firing shots all over the place. If, however, he is white with shock and stares sightlessly before him he could be dangerous because he won't think to clear the weapon and by the time you arrive he could be firing shots all over the place. This one was white and staring and I regarded him therefore as potentially dangerous. His friend lay on the floor, a 9mm. bullet in his thigh. They were *vedettes*.

The Oxford Dictionary Fifth Edition 1964 definition of *vedette* is, 'mounted sentry placed in advance of an outpost.' The vedettes in Intaf weren't allowed near the horses, were never sentries, were the last to go anywhere, and we had no outposts, at least as you will understand them. Some twerp in our head office had doubtless heard the term in a quiz programme (half the ministry couldn't spell it let alone visualise it in place), had sped, I imagine, up the stairs with it to the twerp at the top who in turn had rushed to His Twerpship, the Minister.

Now the Minister would not know whether we used horses or camels, had outposts or inposts. No matter. The name received the royal stamp of approval and we were stuck with it. Vedettes were simply men doing their call-up duty and were usually posted to Protected Villages where they sat on their arses, unless they had medical certificates to say they suffered from piles, or gout, or single testicularity or whatever other debilitating afflictions, in which case they remained in Darwin and answered the radio or did bar duty or cleaned the lavatories or sat on their arses or whatever. We would get some forty odd of these odd sods at any one time, for six-week spells, and while some were good and some were bad, when I cast my mind back to those days it is swept aside somehow by a sea of memories all seemingly ugly.

Back to our A.D.

Not wanting, this Monday morning, a bellyful of 9mm. parabellum on top of office tea, I was rapidly working out my tactics, and having decided on the mundane approach: act bored, just passing the time of day casually, as if saying – 'I see Arsenal won' – I would say something like: 'I see you've shot your mate, then,' which is what I decided I would say. So . . .

'I see you've shot your mate, then,' says I.

It's called psychology. It's strange how the ordinary can occupy one's mind in times of crisis, like noticing that the headmaster has a bogy up his nose as he prepares to thrash you to ribbons with the school cat. And as I stood there waiting for a reaction I remember thinking, 'God. Monday morning. Just had the armoury floor swept and swabbed and here's this bastard dripping blood all over it.'

'Right,' says I, fed up. 'Give me the pistol.' It was still aimed at the groaning heap of misery on the floor. I repeated the order and it was numbly handed over. A crowd was beginning to gather so I handed the whole bloody scene over to Barry, an S.D.O., bless him, and walked back up the stairs.

At the top I met Mrs. H. who I suppose was my secretary; the D.C. had his own. Her cheerful cockney face was sundered through by undisguised merriment.

'Monday morning's gone off with a bang, then,' says she.

I walked into my office and quietly examined the pistol. It was, as I knew it must be, still fully loaded.

Some vedettes came to be regarded as regulars so often did they return to Darwin and such a one was Doom, a banker somewhere, I think, in real life. Doom's company, as anyone with a faster metabolic rate than a fossil will testify, was enervating, sent you to sleep, even in overdrive, and if I saw him bearing down on me I hid in the lav, and locked the door until he had gone. Everything about him was mechanical. His movements, while those of the robot, were not those of your ordinary robot, but of the extra-terrestrial super-model, a voice having been installed that was both slow and resonant and thought processes that, if somewhat cumbersome, were at least obedient. Doom didn't wear a bolt through his neck, but I wouldn't have been surprised to discover that he was got going with an aluminium key. His own name he regarded as classified information and to this day I do not know what it was.

Communication with Doom was an art form, a precious thing one lingered lovingly over, like an ice-cold beer or a glass of vintage wine, English sausage and chips wrapped in the sports page of the Times. He was never in a hurry.

'Where is the D.C?' you ask, not that you want to know, and instead of getting, say – 'The D.C. has gone out in his Land Rover with the S.D.O. to visit a P.V.' - you got, if you hung round long enough: 'The Delta Charlie has gone out in his Lima Romeo with the Sierra Delta Oscar to visit a Papa Victor.'

Doom took half an hour to order a Bravo Echo Echo Romeo.

Now in those days we lived in a row of Intaf houses on what was known as 'The Ridge' about a mile north of Darwin, and the first night we were shot at, guess who was on radio duty in the Ops. Room? We had gone to bed. As the shooting started I ushered my wife and children into the corridor, believed to be as safe as anywhere, and went to the dining room where I kept the radio.

'Ops. Room,' I shout into the darkness, for it was noisy.

'Ops. Room, over.' The voice of, no it couldn't be, Doom.

'Doom. Seagull, over.' Seagull, alias me. Soaring on wings of dread.

'Yes, sir, over.'

'Doom. We're being fired at, over.'

'Yes, sir. I have reported automatic fire to Delta Charlie, over.'

Good old Doom. The instructions on the Ops. Room Board read, 'In case of attack inform D.C. immediately.' It was STEP ONE. He hadn't belted (I doubt in all fairness he knew how to belt. He wouldn't in any case have been programmed for belting.) across to J.O.C. (Joint Operations Committee) to find out what they knew and if, which was all I wanted to know, they were reacting.

'So you've reported it to the D.C. have you, Doom, over?'

'Yes, sir, over.'

'Well done, Doom, over.'

'Thank you, sir, over.'

'How's the family, Doom, over?'

'Fine thank you, sir, over.'

'And the children, over?'

'Very well thank you, sir, over.'

'Doom, over.'

'Yes sir, over.'

'So you've reported it to the D.C., have you, Doom, over?'

'Yes, sir, over.'

'THE D.C. ISN'T BLOODY WELL BEING SHOT AT, OVER.' Calm down. Mental throttling movements. Cough. 'Doom, could you please get me a few details about the shooting, over?'

Short silence while thought processes occupied his circuits. Then, he asks, 'Should I speak with Sunray, Juliet Oscar Charlie, over?' It was STEP TWO.

Someone was crawling between my legs. My wife, Sandra.

'What the hell are you doing?' I ask.

'Looking for fags,' says she. Jesus. I'm being mown down by hails of tracer bullets and she's looking for fags. At least she's keeping her head. She and Doom both.

'Yes,' I yell at Doom. I had pictures of him traipsing mechanically across to J.O.C., telling their Radio Operator (Pronto), in code, all he knew while Pronto lapsed into a deep coma, traipsing back. I gave him five minutes.

'Ops. Room, over.'

'Yes, sir, over.'

'Have you informed army, over?'

'Yes, sir, over.'

'Are they reacting, over?'

'Don't know, sir, over.'

I hear my oldest daughter, Cathy, who is eleven, yelling at her younger brother and sister not to sit on the cold floor. 'You'll get piles. Sit on the carpet.' Three people keeping their heads, even if Doom's did sit precariously on his shoulders.

'WELL BLOODY WELL FIND OUT.'

Moments later a fully informed D.O. (he had done what Doom should have done) came on the radio, thank God, and when the din had died down we all went back to bed.

The story came out the following day. The Roads Camp to the north of us was guarded by coloured troops and they, having seen shadows to their south, had opened up. This had started the Cypriot shopkeepers off, which had started Intaf horse troop off, which had started the police off which had started everyone off.

A couple of nights later it started again but we turned over, over, jammed the pillows over our ears, and went back to sleep. So we missed the real one. Not that that mattered. I couldn't have faced another night of Doom.

Communication, if one let one's guard down, could deteriorate into something less preferable than smoke-signals. Gaps would appear out of nowhere and before you knew it disaster had paid a call.

Barry, the S.D.O., however, once tried building a bridge across a gap in communication where in fact no gap existed.

One intake of vedettes that came sauntering down the trail to Darwin comprised recent immigrants from Mozambique, all of whom, surprise, were medically certified. So, being unable to send them into the bush where they would get themselves killed, we did the next best thing and handed them over to Barry who had a degree in psychology. Barry, however, for all his patience, seemed unable to get through to them. He would spend hours in his office explaining their several duties to them but the harder he tried to make himself understood the more he seemed to fail. Believing, despite all the evidence, in his fellow man, Barry attributed this impasse to shortcomings in his own ability to communicate. He would stand them at ease in his office and say,

'You, erm, you go Radio Room. Hey? Radio Room.'

They would smile at each other, shrug their shoulders, slouch against the desk, against the walls and one another, and thrust out their palms as if warming them against the flames of Rome or a woman's backside.

This frustrated Barry, so he would send them to their quarters to lie down, a discipline in which they had all acquired masters degrees. If he who had a thing in psychology couldn't get through, let them eat cake.

I learned, through a colleague, of Barry's communication problems regarding these heaps of undecorative, inedible exotics and, button-holing the fellow one morning in the corridor, taught him a couple of things about psychology that no longer form part of the curriculum.

In their first couple of weeks at Darwin our Portuguese brethren had become part of the furniture, sloppy furniture, furniture that hawked and spat and smoked non-stop, furniture that slouched against anything upright and grimaced with pain whenever anyone passed them by, but furniture nevertheless. Then one day, no furniture.

'Where Portuguese brethren?' I asked Barry, and he explained his communication problem. 'They're bone bloody idle, man,' says I. 'Surely you can see that.'

'No,' says Barry. 'Just don't understand English.' A brief tactical discussion ended with Barry promising, 'O.K. We'll put it to the test.'

Now for quite some time we had intended building a dog-dip. For the uninitiated, a dog-dip is a concrete-lined hole in the ground filled with water and tick-killer. You throw your dog in one end and when he emerges at the other, hey presto, ticklessness. More or less. It's a big hole and it has to be dug.

'Right Barry. Stick shovels and picks in their hands, show them where to dig, point your finger at them, indicate the picks and shovels, put in a few sound effects, grunt, groan, fart, whatever you like, but don't dig the bloody hole for them.'

I watched from one of the offices. There they stood, idleness incarnate, shrugging and looking bewildered. I watched Barry indicate how they were to tote that barge, lift that bale, watched him take a pick and show them how to extract music from its seemingly inarticulate exterior, watched him illustrate the magical properties of shovel-dig-deeply, watched one reluctant hero start forward in pain as Barry further illustrated the shovel's versatility, watched vedettes start digging.

It took them a week to dig that dip; a job two healthy males would do in a day. Healthy. Ah. They took it in turns to go off sick, go to the doctor, go to bed, return groaning, go off sick. Or they went shopping. Apart from going off sick, lying in bed, and groaning, the only activity capable of stimulating their interest and holding it for more than twenty seconds seemed to be shopping. Even when they weren't shopping they went shopping. It's the Mediterranean blood, I guess.

When they had finished the dip and Barry had them in his office, he was delighted to discover in them a pleasantly surprising grasp of the English language, that they had somehow made themselves familiar with expressions like 'Radio Room', 'Sentry Duty' and 'Bone idle bastards'. What they'd done was spend every minute God gave them (provided Barry didn't then take it away) tirelessly unraveling the intricacies of English grammar and syntax, and thumbing their way through well-worn Oxford dictionaries. We were quite proud of them.

This animal has a tail however. One of their company had written (in English) a letter to the S.I.A. complaining of their treatment. The S.I.A. sent a rocket back by return of post and I was summoned by the D.C. to attend a ballocking. The Portuguese, wrote the S.I.A., were recent immigrants merely trying to make their contribution to the national effort and were to be treated with respect due. Someone, said, the S.I.A., had called them 'Bloody Porks.'

'Now then,' says the D.C. 'Who called these Bloody Porks "Bloody Porks"?'

I smiled at him, shrugged my shoulders, slouched against his desk, and thrust out my palms as if warming them against the flames of Rome or a woman's backside.

Though most Portuguese vedettes were of an undeniably delicate disposition which manifested itself in fainting fits whenever words such as 'work' or 'bush' were mentioned, one Portuguese vedette of another, later, intake received with calm equanimity the news that he was to go out in a Land Rover with Dave, the D.O. at Pachanza P.S.O. who now takes pictures of nude females for Scope magazine.

On their first day together however they hit a landmine, a boosted one, meaning it had other explosives packed down with it. So when the Land Rover took off from the blast, it flew, with the greatest of ease, some fifteen yards or so.

Dave and his Portuguese companion were immediately brought into Darwin for medical treatment, and though Dave was back at work a day later, apparently unscathed, it didn't nudge the earth off its axis when the vedette reported sick with an injured back and retired to bed. A day or so later he came to see me, groaning as was their wont, and asked to go to Salisbury to see his daughter. I couldn't see how, apart from providing him with sympathy and affection neither of which he got in Darwin, his daughter could help, and sent him thus unconsoled back to bed. Following day, 'Want to see daughter' groaning. Back to bed.

Next day back again, this time with a friend, a pleasant fellow who believed there might be a communication problem. I waited a few moments as they jabbered away in Pork and at the end of it the friend says -

'No, he doesn't want to see his *daughter*. He wants to see his doctor.'

CHAPTER 5
BARRY

Here's a bit of nonsense if you like. But first . . .

When God made this, His perfect universe, He managed somehow, for one infinitesimal moment, which was long enough, to fumble the ball and made creatures that were flawed. He intended to destroy these creations but Satan got to them first and used them to recreate chaos. They come to us in the guise of politicians and journalists, and it is the latter of the two that now force their way into this, my hitherto innocent narrative. Journalists I met by their hundreds in Darwin and, remembering that their western masters would only have sent the fag-ends of the journalistic world to report on places like Rhodesia and with every respect due to all the respectable ones neither I nor anyone else has ever met, it behoves me to point out that I found them to be arrogant, self-opinioned which is a dispositional birth-mark, treacherous, illiterate, blind to any fact that flies in the face of their ill-informed, simplistic conceptions, and as thick as pig-shit.

And anyway, it is a mistake to apply standards of any nature to people whose sole satanic purpose is simply to destroy standards.

For instance - it had been got about in Salisbury that Something Big had taken place in Darwin and we were informed by some H.Q. functionary that a bunch of these blinkered booze-bashers was flying up to report it. The D.C. delegated the task of meeting them to me and I delegated it to Barry. What I said was -

'Barry. I have a little job for you. When these pricks arrive from Salisbury, give them the usual bull-shit and get rid, there's a good fellow,' not knowing that half a dozen of them were sitting there listening.

I expected a smack on the snout, a boot up the butt, something, anything, and I would have been at peace with it, but these lads weren't like that. They simply slid snake-like into dark little holes, soaked Rhodesia in their venom and splashed it all over the front pages of their hellish papers.

The 'Something Big', we discovered, was in reality nothing to write about, no scandal, nothing scurrilous, to slake the evil thirst of our reptilian riffraff – just a mundane multiple murder in one of the villages, a few mutilated bodies, women, children, stuff like that. So our pressmen, immediately losing interest, snorted, made out their reports, and got the hell back to Salisbury. Where, having recharged their pens with poison like the snakes they were, they doubtless repaired to the pub.

Anyway. That bit of nonsense. If you were asked, 'Do you know where the D.C. is?' and you replied -

'He's just gone out with the Secretary for Internal Affairs, the Provincial Commissioner, the Assistant District Commissioner, a couple of Senior District Officers, the Primary Development Officer, a Field Assistant and an Agricultural Officer to visit some Protected Villages, pick up a few District Security Assistants and take them to a Protected Sub-office to hand them over to the District Officer.'

By the time you got it all out, the fellow asking the question would be sleeping in his chair while the spiders made webs in his armpits. So, as if to aid matters, it was all abbreviated and became -

'The D.C.'s out with the S.I.A., the P.C., the A.D.C., a couple of S.D.O.s, the P.D.O., an F.A. and an A.O., to visit some P.V.s, pick up a few D.S.A.s, take them to a P.S.O. and hand them over to the D.O.' Old hat. (Doom of course would create a peroration of his reply and before he was done even the spiders would have their feet up and newspapers over their faces.)

The stage is more or less set, it lacking but a couple of actors, preferably clowns. One afternoon a journalist walked into my office. He had an appointment with the D.C. who, blessed with a memory able to dismiss matters of no or very little consequence from its presence, such as appointments with politicians and journalists and other people of no consequence, had forgotten said appointment, full stop. We exchanged mutually suspicious greetings and he asked after the D.C.

'I think,' says I, 'he's gone out with the S.I.A. the P.C. and a couple of S.D.O.s, the P.D.O. and the A.O. to visit one of the P.V.s,' and carried on working. Sort that lot out, thinks I, smug as a skunk.

'Erm,' he coughs. 'Do you know what time he'll be back?'

I said I thought about 15:30.

'O.K. I'll wait.'

I went to Barry's office and asked him to get on the radio and find out where the D.C. was and what his E.T.A. I also asked a favour. On his return Barry says to the poor sod in the waiting room,

'Is it you has an appointment with the D.C.?'

'Yes, it is.'

'I'm afraid,' says Barry, 'he's gone out with the S.I.A. the P.C....' and so on.

'Thank you,' says The Father of Original Thought, aware that a rare variety of piss was being taken.

O.K. Barry was primed. But the D.C. wasn't. As he walked towards his office, showering dust over everyone, he poked his head into the waiting room and said,

'Sorry I'm late,' with weary authority, his nose having been recalled to the grindstone by Barry. 'But I had to take the P.C. a couple of S.D.O.s, the P.D.O. and an A.O. to one of the P.S.O.s. Would you like to come in?'

'Thank you,' I heard him reply, and as the door was closing, 'Actually, I've just been up to Mtoko visiting P.V.s with the A.D.C. and the P.D.O. Most interesting.' The journalist, in other words, had just returned from his duty as a vedette in a neighbouring district. Dear Lord, the bugger was one of ours.

Barry was a wiry, hyper-active fellow with specs, hair scraped forward like a balding Roman, and by any known standards of measurement, 13, say, on the Richter Scale - mad. Some of the stuff he read for psychology had begun to rub off. When I first arrived in Darwin he was the D.O. at Mukumbura P.S.O. and was affectionately, I think is the right word, known as the Mayor of Muckers. He had his own Flag of Independence which he'd designed and printed himself and which flew proudly over the camp, and if you wished to get in you had to apply for one of his visas. Prime Minister or tramp, no visa no entry.

I had been sent up there one afternoon to show a couple of ladies around, and Barry thought it might be nice to take them to the Surf Club for lunch.

O.K.

Surf Club? I hear you say. But there was a war on, grown men despaired, maidens miscarried, fruit rotted on the branch, crops wilted and withered away.

The Surf Club was so called because Mukumbura fronted on the Mukumbura River separating Rhodesia from Portuguese East, as it was then and ever shall be, amen, and one could theoretically therefore go surfing, but I have never seen water in the river, even during the rainy season, and I always remember Mukumbura as a sun-blasted expanse of loveless scrub, a place of dust and emptiness.

The club, alias pub, Barry had built with the help of a few derelict policemen and other scoundrels, using materials that belonged, and this is now recorded for the first time, to someone else. There were, in Darwin itself, some twelve pubs all of which, when the final coat of paint had been applied, belonged to associations, clans, fraternities or messes, but which, broken down into their component parts, belonged to someone else.

The Surf Club was an underground affair (mortar bombs, old chap) and one gained access to it by a short flight of steps, sleepers, in fact, kindly donated – people were very kind in those days, you know – by Rhodesia Railways. Barry led the way down the steps, the ladies followed, and I brought up the rear, and as we stopped in the threshold I was immediately captivated by the enchantment of its interior. I found myself smiling with surprise, O.K. relief, at the cosy atmosphere caring people had wrought. So, I thought, this is the famous Surf Club … and one of the ladies beside me gasped,

'What a beau … ' and she pulled up sharply in her tracks.

The eye, after taking in, as it does with a well-organised painting, the main focal point, the focal point here being tastefully covered easy chairs, would move across the floor and upwards where it would come to rest on the polished wooden bar and the personal mugs at the rear, then, glancing sideways, the wall-lighting dim and inviting, then crash, it fell upon an object hanging from a beam that was instantly identifiable.

This was Barry's cock-warmer, a small article of clothing knitted in the very image of the male pendularia and worn by Eskimos when fishing in iceholes. Barry would never tell you who had made it for him and you didn't question him too closely lest it be your wife.

But that was Barry. Mad. As all serious students of psychology should be. That afternoon I watched him about his business. The ladies had flown back to Darwin and I was to return by Land Rover via Chigango P.S.O. where I would spend the night – I used to agree to these things being the rookie, but I discovered one day they could be dangerous and thereafter employed Churchillian principles to show how great administration understands the what, when and how of delegation.

Anyway. About that afternoon – the still, baking air, cicadas blaring away down by the river, toiling gangs of African labourers squabbling intermittently and wandering off for a wee, D.S.A.s quietly polishing boots beneath the occasional shady tree, the hum of persistent flies, and bearing all before it Barry's imperious voice crying,

'Tshonalanga, you bastards. Tshonalanga.'

It was his favourite call to victory. It came from the Zulu 'Ilanga litshonile' (I think, and who in hell will know the difference) meaning, 'The sun has gone down'. See a gang of labourers slackening at the shovel and off he would go, head bent forward and crying as he bore down on them,

'Tshonalanga, you bastards,' good naturedly, because for reasons beyond the comprehension of ordinary mortals he was fond of the idle devils, and they in turn would smile at each other behind their shovels and jab fingers at their heads. 'Cos he was mad and they knew it.

During proceedings, whether it was the same day or not I cannot remember and is anyway immaterial, one day in Barry's life being much the same as any other, a truck arrived from Darwin bearing a dozen or whatever coffins, and when the D.S.A.s utterly refused to off-load them – something to do with an ancient African superstition dating back into the misty beginnings of Rhodesia's war with terrorism – Barry dug deep into the well of his psychic resources, fell in, more like, and blundered around in the deep dark recesses of that other world about him, the mysterious world of psychology, and when he resurfaced came up with,

'Tshonalanga you bastards. Tshonalanga. We bought them for you. You get 'em off,' at which they ran from him wailing and hid down latrines 'til he took his nonsense elsewhere.

Mukumbura was the site of the first P.V. ever installed in the country, and in 1973 I had had a hand in setting it up. So on my return I was interested to see what it was like with people settled there. Barry gave me a guided tour.

The Chief's hut had the word 'Chief' and his name conspicuously displayed on the outside, the Headman's hut, 'Headman' and his name, Kraalheads the same, and their people trailed anonymously in long lines of huts. Toilets had been installed but they seemed to be little used.

'Ah,' says Barry. 'Put pigs in a sty and the first thing they will do is choose a corner to shit in. This lot shit where it suits.'

I didn't argue. He was a farmer's son.

'But why?' says I perturbed.

I remember as a boy, being desperate one evening and miles from the nearest lavatory, creeping into a churchyard and relieving myself among the tombstones, and in the hereafter I will doubtless be turned into a dungbeetle and made to roll a ball up a hill like Sisyphus. His rock rolled rhythmically back down again whenever he reached the summit. My mortal punishment, had I been caught by the local bobby, would have been a sharp clout round the ear and another when I got home, because crapping in churchyards is uncivilised.

I asked Reg, one of our accountants,

'When you were a P.O.W., Reg, did you crap more or less where you liked?'

'Course.'

'Eh?'

'Well,' says Reg. 'I don't know about you but I *like* to crap in the lav.'

'Ah.'

'Look. The Eye-tyes deliberately tried to degrade you. Take away your self-respect. You didn't try to make it easy for them, did you?'

The P.V. at Mukumbura had been supplied with rubbish bins, which stood at the end of each kraal-line, but they were hardly used. Everywhere I looked I was reminded of the shop-fronts owned by the Greek Cypriots in Darwin – fruit-peel, beer-packets, boxes, turds.

'Why?' says Barry, slipping in odd 'Tshonalangas' for the benefit of the people he thought should be picking up the rubbish. 'I'll tell you why. The attitude of the inhabitants isn't, "Well, let's make the best of it while we're here," but, "Well, we'll be out of here in the next twenty or thirty years so why bother".'

They were allowed out, as it happened, some nine years later when they had expressed their desires through a vote, but by then many of them didn't want to leave. Because what had been created, witlessly or with malice aforethought, was a Growth Point surrounded by wire. All one hears of today in Africa is Growth Point this and Growth Point that, Growth Points being considered the answer to Africa's urban problems. (They aren't, by the way.) And hoary old places like London began their lives as Growth Points, also surrounded, but by walls.

The people in Mukumbura P.V. didn't have two problems to rub together. If their crops failed the government fed them, the school was barely yards away, shops, pubs, ditto. They didn't have to walk miles for water because it was laid on. And no one molested them. On the contrary, they were pampered. Barry piped music to them all day – African dance music that has no rhyme, reason, plot or plan, and like that Scots muck played by Jimmy Shand goes on and on until, as suddenly as it started, thank the Lord, it stops. When a Jimmy Shand record comes to an end I am filled with so overwhelming an inner release I want to go round kissing all my fellow creatures. The Scots feel the same way while it's playing. That should tell you something. Ancient land rights had nothing to do with Flodden.

Journalists would describe P.V.s with untempered glee as the slums and for reptilian reasons blame us. The land was virgin before people moved in. London is also a slum, but as I say it also began its life as a Growth Point. And that should tell you a great deal.

Before leaving for Chigango I asked Barry if he would please bless the wheels of my vehicle. Laugh as much as you like but this ritual guaranteed your vehicle immunity against the activities of landmines and see you safely home.

Think for a moment on those old westerns where the heroine is roped to a totem pole while hordes of natives prance about and propitiate the spirits before they cut her up and fed her to the dogs. They never did get to cut her up of course because the script had to make room for acts of heroism that spoiled everyone's fun. Anyway.

Thus it was with Barry. Taking up his ancient fly-whisk he would wallawalla-whisky the vehicle, chant mystic mumbo-jumbo known only to himself and the gods of locomotion, prance and jerk and writhe, then, suddenly convulsing, lash the outer tyre with the fly-whisk and pluck from the air above him magical powers that ran through his arms, through the fly-whisk, and through to the dark tube within. He didn't froth at the mouth but it wasn't for want of trying and when he had finished your wheels, imbued with his special powers, could sense, as they bounced and thumped along the dreadful bloody roads, the presence of landmines several miles ahead and would leap high in the air and out of danger, like someone in the bush suddenly coming upon a snake.

When Barry first started this blessing stunt people laughed good-humouredly and jabbed fingers at their heads knowing he was mad, but it became a regular feature, good for morale. (Psychologist, you see.) Then one day, Barry is away visiting another P.S.O., an unblessed convoy of vehicles leaves Mukumbura, two miles down the road 'scerrboom'. The laughter of sceptics was tinged with fidgeting uncertainly thereafter and I for one would refuse to leave Mukumbura until Barry had done his stuff with the flywhisk. This doesn't mean he wasn't mad, because he was.

CHAPTER 6

OUR BELOVED MINISTER

It was an open secret that our beloved Prime Minister regarded the Ministry of Internal Affairs with suspicion, loathing and contempt, and the Minister he gave us, even by the high standards set by politicians, was an incompetent lout who should never have been allowed near a cement-mixer let alone a portfolio. On very rare occasions, thank goodness, he flew up to Darwin to talk to the staff and boost morale, morale that only waned on those rare occasions when he flew up to Darwin to talk to staff and boost morale. He was English, you might know. Paid by the British Exchequer.

You are a fly on the wall of the Prime Minister's office. He is about to appoint our Minister.

'Ah. Come in, dunderhead.'

'Thank you, Prime Minister.'

'Sit down, twerp.'

'Thank you, Prime Minister.'

'Now see here. You're an incompetent bungler.'

'Yes, Prime Minister.'

'So we're giving you Internal Affairs. Think you can screw it up?'

'Oh yes, Prime Minister. Certainly, Prime Minister. Thank you, Prime Minister.'

'Good. Off you go then. Balls it all up.'

'Immediately, Prime Minister.'

'Oh. And you can start with Mt. Darwin. Things are going far too well up there.'

'Don't you worry, Prime Minister.'

My task it is to pick him up at the airfield. The S.I.A. is with him, basking in reflected glory. Indeed, as I drive, the rays that emanate from His Omnifulgence light up the whole cab. He turns his light on me,

'How are things in Mt. Darwin, Mr. er...?'

'Fine thank you, Minister.'

'How long have you been here now, Mr. er…?'

'About twelve months, Minister.' I whistle.

'Are you happy here, Mr. er…?'

He has an army of civil servants, great lumbering divisions, to do his research for him but knowing everything he hasn't bothered to use them. Ten minutes later I drop His Omniscience off in the D.C.'s office and summon the staff for the meeting. This first meeting is for office staff only – some twenty odd people ranging in age from young cadet D.O.s of eighteen to our two accountants, Jack and Reg, who are in their sixties, are 39/45 British war veterans and have retired only recently from the army. They are hard nuts to crack, having seen a couple of things. Some members of staff have university degrees, many can speak more than one language, and a few wear decorations for gallantry.

Our Minister is a carpenter catapulted to eminence by politics. As Reg would say, it takes two years to make a good soldier but you can become a Minister overnight.

'Now,' says His Omnipresence after a few languid comments about the weather. 'I would like to begin by talking about P.V.s. This doesn't concern you people, I know, as you don't have any.'

The S.I.A. whispers in his ear.

'Oh?' says His Omnipotence.

He and the S.I.A. have been strapped together in an aeroplane for three-quarters of an hour between Salisbury and Darwin. What, one wonders, do our gods talk about when perched on Olympus?

'Where are we then?' and a conspiratorial wink, intimating that, what with his impish interior and the pressures of a busy schedule, on the move all the time, don't yer know, he was some sort of a guy and we were lucky if we got a hand to the hem of his robe.

'Mt. Darwin,' says the S.I.A., getting it spot on.

'Oh, then it does concern you.' No apologies. Only mortals apologise. As he's incapable of getting something as basic as P.V.s right, everyone loses interest and nods off. The D.C. and I want desperately to join them but daren't lest the jerk sitting between us ask us questions which he won't because he knows everything.

The evening was memorable. We had arranged to hold the second meeting in the Intaf pub, 'The Changamire Arms', where the Minister would address himself to the D.O.s and other members of staff from the P.S.O.s who had come into Darwin especially to hear him.

The Changamire Arms belonged, in spirit, to Intaf, Darwin. It consisted of two linking corrugated iron water-tanks, previously on the books of Water Development. These had been given an inch-thick covering of cement and from the outside looked very like a pair of binoculars standing on end. The bar was in one tank, the lounge in the other, and they gave access unto each other via an interconnecting door. You could therefore see from the bar into the lounge and the whole thing, thanks to unofficial funds, had a pleasant, homely feel about it. The roof was thatched, creeper grew up the walls, and there was a small lawn enclosed by wooden palings. It lived a few yards behind the D.C.'s offices and was the focal point of Intaf activity.

The Minister sat in the lounge up against a small window so that he could see through to the bar in whose dark corners all our lower life, Geordie, Yarra, and Bill, lurked and listened and waited for the scraps. His glass of ambrosia sat on a small, mahogany coffee table while we unworthy mortals sat adoringly on the floor or in easy chairs before him. A log fire (it was winter) blazed in the hearth.

He began with African Councils.

Since about the middle forties, if I remember rightly, Africans in the Tribal Areas had been encouraged by the Department of Native Affairs, later Internal Affairs, to run their own show. The concept of the African Council had as its model the British Local Authority, a microcosm, that is, of the democratic state, but because it is hopelessly alien to African cultural, historical, and socio-economic heritage it invariably failed.

Council was encouraged from time to time to take over from the Native Commissioner, later District Commissioner, responsibilities for schools, clinics, roads, water, more or less everything.

The D.C. or a member of his senior staff was President of council, sat on all its meetings in order to ensure that the requirements of the intricate African Councils Act were met and provide general guidance. The budget, for example, was prepared by the Council Secretary but the D.C. went through it with him to ensure its accuracy and/or viability. D.C.'s staffs were on tap to assist where and when they were asked. Simple.

Sooner or later, however, Council would experience – I worked with some twenty councils throughout the country and there were no exceptions – one or all of the following problems.

First, the people refused to pay their rates so that budget figures became meaningless and nothing therefore, or very little, was accomplished. Schools fell to pieces, clinics ground to a halt, ditto everything else, and only beer outlets which generated their own funds survived. Capital Works remained a figment of the budget's imagination and the people complained that council did nothing for them. So they refused to pay their rates. Hands up those people who spotted a vicious circle.

Second, the Secretary was bone idle and did nothing and/or seemed unable to distinguish council money from his own. So the people became disillusioned.

Third, the councillors weren't interested. The people didn't know what if anything was going on. Independent Africa writ small, I hear the cynics say.

Areas in independent Zimbabwe where the people have been made to resuscitate their councils are ruled by chaos and his twin brother corruption, and a Great Plan has emerged to join them up with white councils that mysteriously manage to thrive.

I could write a book.

Now, Prime Minister apart, anyone with the brains of a dray-horse agreed – look at your history books – that the platform for successful counter measures in a war against terrorism can only be provided by good administration. Remove administration and terrorism takes over. I have discussed this with top, middle, and lower brass of many organisations, civil and military, and though they may disagree with my choice of toilet-paper or my views regarding the cultural implications of the Peloponnesian War, they all agree about good administration.

'Gentlemen,' our Minister began, 'We are looking at the moment at handing over administration in places like, er, well, Mt. Darwin to

African Councils.' Whoa there. This whiffed of Ian Smith because, say what you liked, and we all did, about Intaf's head office, even they weren't that stupid. Stupid yes, oh, so stupid the mind boggled: they unwittingly condensed and purified the word stupid, created of it an art form, but honestly not that stupid. And I could think of no-one else, no flying saucers had landed in the previous twenty-four hours, who would give the idea enough oxygen to generate.

The unprecedented imbecility of the idea seemed to hit everyone simultaneously – even our cadet D.O.s who wouldn't know the difference between an African Council and a tumescent donkey, or a Tumescent Council and an African donkey, were heard to gasp. Something else hit them. If councils took over it was goodbye job. Skeletal D.C. staff. Definitely Smith.

At the bar, though not officially part of the meeting, sat, as I say, Geordie, Yarra and Bill, and as I had parked myself up against the interconnecting door I was able to eavesdrop on their conversation as the Minister prated on. There were none of the Minister's big words, but the critical monosyllabic assessments emanating from the bar were more eloquent, more honourable, and made more sense than anything coming out of the lounge.

'Wanker,' loudly from Geordie.

'Crap,' sleepily, from Yarra. Succinct. I liked it.

The Minister drivelled on. We weren't, he said, to worry because there would be more work not less, more jobs not fewer. Meanwhile, back at the bar,

'Bum,' Bill, Irishly.

'Wanker,' becoming more vehement.

'Craap,' becoming, 'Craaap,' then, 'Craaaap,' sleepily, sheepily.

When His Omnificence had finished I, feeling the effects of a long, bad day, asked a couple of desultory questions intended merely to irritate the Minister and the D.C. quietly tore him apart. This was the cue for Barry, bulldozing.

We had been begging Head Office for years for rational supplies of weaponry and equipment. D.S.A.s were armed with 303s which, while fine rifles, were no match for the sophisticated, automatic AK 47 used by Russians, we had enough radios for ten men when we needed a hundred, and so on. The whole bang-shoot was less convincing than one of Geordie's expletives. Everyone hates losing men and none more than Barry who was forever bitching about supplies. He now bitched to the Minister, who gave him the old,

'See what we can do.'

'Heard it all before,' says Barry. 'Thousands of times.'

This opened up the floodgates, releasing great quantities of pent-up energy and the D.O.s now roared through like a river in flood drowning the Minister in great tidal waves of frustration and anger. When, to mix metaphors injudiciously, the debris, dust and smoke had cleared away, the Minister says,

'I am disappointed to find the Darwin morale at such a low ebb.'

Remember morale?

Barry, now mad with injured pride, catapulted from his seat, marched up to the coffee-table, and said to His Omnibus,

'One more remark like that and I'll smash your stupid face in.'

At which, knowing that nothing, as usual, would be done to alleviate the problems, the rest of us lost all interest and retired to the bar. I can still see Geordie's face, red and fierce, as I approached.

'But he's a f.....g wanker, Rob,' says Geordie, and Yarra, half asleep with his feet up, going, 'Craaaap.'

I had to – had to – dine at the D.C.'s house that evening, and His Omnivorous became so drunk that he came up with a memorable remark, doubtless the only one he's ever made. And I was there to witness it. A Spoonerism.

The D.C. kept fish on the verandah, and the Minister, because he kept fish himself, says,

'It's an expensive piece of equipment, a taught ter wank.'

And that did my morale the world of good.

CHAPTER 7

SONS OF GLENDOWER

Mike was one of our Agricultural Officers. I have mentioned the creeper along the walls of the Changamire Arms. Mike planted the seeds of this stuff but when a few days later it poked its head out of the ground it was obvious, even to Mike, that something seriously ailed it. It clearly didn't like the cruel, harsh world in which it found itself, went completely off its food and refused to grow any further. No matter how much love and affection Mike bestowed upon it he could not coax it out of its deep melancholy state. And then, one week, Mike went away on leave.

It began immediately to climb up the walls, it was happy and vibrant, sang its silly head off, rejoiced in the warmth of the day, so that when Mike returned he was delighted. A few days later, however, it began mysteriously to wilt. To droop forlornly. We could never understand this. Whenever Mike was around it would give up and start to turn brown but as soon as he was away it would thrive.

There was something about Mike that Flora just didn't take to and if he entered a room they would turn their backs on him and whisper in little groups. Buy a bag of mushroom spawn. Let Mike water it painstakingly for months and nothing will appear. Let him go away for a week and mushrooms take over the house. They lift the roof off its moorings, smash their way through windows and doors, and wave to people passing by. Some Agricultural Officer. He manages a farm somewhere now, so that's had it.

Mike had some thirty black agricultural staff within his jurisdiction and if he thought they were being ill-treated, even by The Holy Trinity, hell, all you needed do was tell them to cut their hair or straighten their ties, and he'd have his hands round your throat and accuse you of being a bloody racist that didn't give a shit about black people.

'You wouldn't treat them like that if they were white,' he'd yell.

Though born in Rhodesia he had inherited Welsh volatility from his parents and reacted predictably to criticism. So I cannot think of Mike without remembering the pistol incident. He kept a 9mm pistol in his desk and one day it went missing. The police were called in but it was hopeless. The pistol re-surfaced some two weeks later, however, when it played the central character to a packed beer-hall during a hold-up in Bindura, a town some seventy kilometres south of Darwin. The weapon was thus recovered and given over to C.I.D. Mike, meanwhile, had problems keeping his bowels quiet, facing, as he was, a possible thousand-dollar fine and even imprisonment.

The member in charge of the case in Darwin was Detective Patrol Officer Taffy – that's right. Muscular and compact, Taffy could have been no more than five and a half feet tall but every inch was hard and unyielding. He had an irrepressible sense of humour and a morbid interest in things expired. Hence C.I.D.

Taffy came to see me and explained how the pistol had been recovered.

'Is Mike in any sort of trouble?' says I.

'No,' says Taffy, off-hand. Then lighting up, 'Tell you what though. Pretend he's up to his neck and send him to see me.'

A little while later I found Mike planting trees upside down and po-faced told him the news.

'Is there going to be,' says he, 'any shit?'

'I think so, yes,' says I. 'Look. If I were you I'd go see Taffy chop-chop and get it sorted out.' I put on a reassuring face and watched Mike's go green. Plants go brown, people green.

I watched him cross the road, hesitate, turn back, stop, make up his mind if he had one left, and wander down to the C.I.D. offices. It was only a hundred yards away. It then went, Taffy told me later, something thus.

Mike knocks on the door.

'Come in.' Stern voice from within. Mike enters. Taffy is typing furiously.

'Morning, Taffy,' which receives a cold and formal -

'Good morning. Please sit down Mr. er . . .' Mike green.

Now you must remember that the previous evening Taffy and Mike have been getting smashed together and singing Welsh rugby songs at the Changamire.

'What seems to be the prob . . . ?' asks Mike.

'Now Mr. erm . . . I have to take a 'Warned and Cautioned' statement from you so if you would please tell me from the beginning how you lost the pistol.'

Mike tells his story while Taffy silently types it out. When the interview is finished Mike, wishing to be elsewhere and quickly, signs the 'Warned and Cautioned' without lingering to read it and shoots from the office. He's in the shit, shit, shit.

Taffy brought the document to my office half an hour later and I have it before me as I write, yellowing with age. The document, that is.

Mike is charged with contraventions of the Mental Disorders Act, CAP 130, is warned that any statement he makes will be written down on paper, screwed up into little balls and used as hair-curlers. He admits to inherent stupidity, being an illiterate and a drunk.

Taffy and I took this piece of incriminating drivel into Mike's office and showed it to him. As he read it through, his face, still tinged about the gills with an evanescent green, started backwards through the spectrum reflecting the fury that began building up within – green, yellow, orange, red. Very, very, very red. His blood, as I say, was imported from Wales.

'Very funny, hey,' says he, jaw-muscles rippling, and Taffy and I left him to stew. He had come off lightly after all.

Welsh furnaces, fed on the finest coal, are long aglow, and for the next few days Mike sat in his office and smouldered. He was determined to get even with Taffy but rack his Welsh brain as he might nothing issued forth. I had an idea.

In order to save foreign currency the government had only months before put a ban on the import of cigarette wrapping. After all, the world used our tobacco, we made our own cigarettes out of floor scrapings, so why not make the wrapping. Out they came, and to the surprise of all and sundry they were diabolical. Because instead of using silver-foil to wrap them in we used re-cycled newspaper. All you could taste was newspaper. It was the greatest anti-smoking campaign ever launched. Trembling eighty-fag-a-day die-hards gave up smoking. People who had never smoked in their lives gave it up. Adverts on radio and television took one puff and gave it up. Peter Stuyvesant were selling at ten dollars a-piece on the black market, and those fortunate enough to come upon such treasure locked themselves behind strong-room doors before lighting up. It was hell.

I walked into Mike's office one morning.

'The Muse of Mischief,' quoth I, 'hath perched upon my shoulder.'

'Huh?'

'I've had an idea,' and I told him. His banks burst with enthusiasm and we let some of the lads in on it.

Dave who now takes pictures of nude females for Scope magazine had a girlfriend in the offices of the national daily, the 'Herald'. Mike rang up this delectable piece and asked her to insert an advert in the paper for him. This duly appeared a few days later. It read:

'Unlimited supplies of Peter Stuyvesant. For orders please ring Mr..... phone number ..... Mt. Darwin, or write P.O. Box ..... Mt. Darwin.'

The name, phone number, and box number were all Taffy's.

Short and simple. But the chaos it caused was galaxies beyond anything we expected.

Taffy started receiving phone calls as he walked into his office that morning. It had most likely been ringing since two a.m. which was when the newspapers hit the Salisbury streets, but Taffy's public would have to be patient.

The first call he put down to one of those inexplicable things that seem to bedevil everyone who owns a phone. The second, following hard on the heels of the first, aroused his suspicions, and the third, seconds later, confirmed them. He started getting mad at the fourth which was silly because –'I'm sorry, sir. We have both been the victims of a practical joke.' - the phone hadn't even warmed up yet. Before the day was though he would be called upon to answer some three hundred such calls –'I'm sorry, sir. We have both been the victims of a practical joke.' - all asking for Peter Stuyvesant.

The Postmaster got to work at 7.30am. By 7.35 he had despatched Taffy his first telegram and by 7.40 his first telex. By 8 o'clock the telegraphic gold rush was on. It was all hands to the pump. Mundane post-office routine was swept aside by rivers of enquiries, and reserve delivery-boys were brought in to channel them off to Taffy's office.

The next day Taffy received a light sprinkling of mail through the post, a couple of hundred post-cards and letters, but it was merely the foreboding of the avalanche that was on its way. And on the third day it came roaring down the mountainside and buried Taffy up to the chin beneath its onslaught. In Intaf meanwhile our small conspiracy noted the appearance in the paper of the advertisement and got on with its daily routine, innocent as acorns, and scarce daring to mention the fact to each other, while worms of curiosity ate us whole.

Jack, the accountant, walked up to my office around 11 o'clock with the news hot in his hand.

'Have you seen the advert,' says he, 'for Peter Stuyvesant in today's paper?' I looked up, feigning disinterest, but scarce daring to breathe.

'Oh?'

'Yes. Taffy's got unlimited supplies, apparently. No doubt, erm, confiscated somewhere.'

'Jesus,' says I, and Jack trundled off – Jack is one of only a couple of people I've ever known who genuinely trundles – having stated it his intention to buy a couple of thousand. When he got there Taffy met him at the door of his office, apparently allowing no one inside. Taffy stared inwardly at the wraith of insanity fast approaching but his voice was firm and outwardly under control. He knew why Jack was there.

'No, I haven't,' he told Jack. 'It's some sort of hoax,' and Jack left.

Now unknown to us, Taffy, after the fifth or whatever phone call, had told his immediate boss, also a long-standing friend of Intaf, what was bedevilling him, and as Taffy finished speaking, one word, the product of similar minds, rang out.

'Intaf.'

They grabbed the paper and found what they sought.

Their comeback was the product of the mind as rich in mischief as hell itself. Geoff, a Detective Inspector, was born in Birmingham and had emigrated to Rhodesia several years earlier. He had a face that glowed with innocence, but behind it lay a mind as fertile, original, devious and perverse as that of Edgar Allen Poe himself. He was a fiend.

Before they could begin the process of retaliation they needed first to make sure that their suspicions were correct. They had to home in on the right target. They sent therefore an underling who was a bit of an actor to the offices of the Herald. There, fitted out with dark glasses and a beard resembling the cataract at Victoria Falls, he approached Dave's girlfriend, flashed something official and menacing (probably a parking ticket) and confided, 'State Security,' but don't look now.

They suspected, he said, a serious breach of currency regulations up in Darwin and she, being a friend of some of the people there, might possible be able to help with their inquiries. They were investigating all possible channels. He didn't mention cigarettes.

Few ordinary people are brave under these circumstances, and she whispered, 'You mean cigarettes?'

He nodded solemnly. She then blew, as it were, the gaff, doubtless scared out of her pretty little wits, and Geoff's ringer returned triumphantly to Darwin.

I have lost the document in my travels but Taffy now received a 'rocket' from top, H.Q. Salisbury, brass, to wit one Chief Superintendent – two down from God – Williams, a detail I have good cause to remember. The rocket named a dozen or so chapters and the odd verse that Taffy, by advertising Stuyvesant through the press, had contravened, and advised Taffy that in view of his previous unsatisfactory record with the department he must now consider his future with the police before he, the Chief Superintendent, considered it for him – an invitation, that is, to resign.

That evening Taffy and Geoff, as was their wont, paid the Changamire a call. The downcast, mournful look on Taffy's face couldn't have been bettered had he been off to his own wedding, while Geoff bore a look of thoughtful concern.

Geoff had a trump card up his sleeve, the bastard, because the Salisbury memorandum mentioned Taffy's previous record with C.I.D., and Taffy's naughty nature, even to Darwin people, was nothing new. A simple illustration. One night in Salisbury, being drunk, penniless and unable to pay for a taxi home, he lay flat out in the middle of a road until someone reported a dead body. His own people then came and picked him up and he spent the rest of the night in one of his own cells.

Now, the only person in Intaf, so far as I knew, aware that such behaviour had put his career in jeopardy was myself. A few months previously Geoff had confided that Darwin was a punishment station for Taffy, well, it was for most, and that if he didn't toe the line he faced the firing squad. Good at his job, but, well, naughty, and Geoff had asked me to keep an eye on him when he was in the Changamire. An eye. You needed, like 'Rumour' in Vergil's Aeneid who had an eye under each feather, eyes in your arse. However . . .

I sat at the end of the bar with Intaf friends and Geoff sidled up to me. He explained the advert for cigarettes in the paper, that he was going round all the Darwin pubs, showing everybody the 'rocket' from Williams, in the hope of finding out who was behind it all. He, Geoff, personally, himself, thought, in his own mind, that the advert was one hell of a good prank, but he had to extricate Taffy from the s-h-one-t. I read, casual but brain on full alert, the document. It had all the trappings – trite cop circumlocution, tortured cop grammar and syntax, the chapters looked right (as they doubtless were for they would rely on my checking them quietly afterwards), the date-stamp, 'H.Q. Salisbury', looked genuine, and the signature, a bold flourish.

'May I? I asked, holding up the document.

'Course,' said Geoff, and I showed it to the rest of the gang.

'Fake,' I thought.

'I wish I could help, Geoff,' I said, 'but none of our guys are responsible for the advert. I'd know if they were. But if I hear anything, I'll let you know,' and I handed the document back to him.

Then, instead of getting splendidly tanked up, as was their wont, they left. Dead miserable.

The gang looked at me.

'Ah, it's all bull-shit,' I said. 'Sit tight.'

A few discreet nights later in they came, Taffy giving weary, mournful cow looks and Geoff all thoughtful concern.

We chatted generally for a while, tossing trivialities back and forth (I remember Geoff being interested in the creative impact of indifference in a functional society), and then Geoff turned to me.

'Have you, er, managed to pick anything up? About Taffy, I mean.'

'Sorry, no,' I replied.

'I think he's had it this time.'

'Sorry about that.'

'We've been to all the pubs and nothing.'

'Somebody, it seems, has it in for Taffy,' and off they went, all of a mizz.

The gang looked at me.

'Bull-shit,' I said, wavering on the edge of something. 'Sit tight.'

There did, however, seem to be something amiss with Taffy. I went to his office on business next morning and the old Taffy was gone. Usually, all one had to do to get a laugh from him was tie somebody's granny to a tree and blow her up, at which Taffy would subside with merriment, tears rolling from his eyes. Nothing I tried seemed to cheer him up and eventually he walked out of the office and went off on his own into the distance. I went to see Geoff.

'Look,' says I, 'I know who was responsible for the advert. I won't say who, but I'll clear it for Taffy.'

He was thrilled. Would I phone up Chief Superintendent Williams on Monday morning and explain Taffy's innocence.

Sure.

The pompous, half-baked bastard I spoke to was unadulterated cop, complete with cockney accent. He was proto-typical 'proceeding in a northerly direction'. Things were said such as -

'Typical Internal Affairs lack of constraint.'

'Inability to discern the potential outcome.'

'Irresponsibility bordering on the criminal.'

And, as he drivelled on, the ghost of every pompous ass that has ever lived seemed to descend from the realms of misty insubstantiality and crystallise in the squalid heap of mortality at the other end of the line. Indignation, anger and frustration, triple offspring of telephonic communication, blew me apart and after hurling rivers of senseless but satisfying abuse at him I slammed down the phone.

'How'd it go?' Geoff asked that afternoon.

'O.K. Fine.'

The following night in they come. Geoff puts a tape-recorder on the bar and turns it on. And there, reproduced with distressing clarity, is my conversation with Williams, complete with obscenities and mutual abuse. He didn't exist of course. There was no such person. Geoff had primed the girl on the exchange at H.Q. to put me through to a friend of his, a Section Officer with an evil streak, and he had the conversation recorded.

They revealed grudgingly the awesome chaos created by the advert, and I have a few telegrams, rescued by Geoff, before me. One, I see, asks for 8,000, another 5,000, 8,000, 30,000 (from an African), one stating,

'Interested in Stuyvesant stop. Supply quantity price to clear stop', from a well-known Indian trader in Salisbury. 'To clear.' Ye gods. Would that we had had them.

But it does prove something, something they who would rid the world of tobacco and its assorted evils forget. Man is merely steam under pressure. A boiler ready to blow. Why, there are butterflies that cannot face life without their daily fix.

A couple of years later Taffy blew his brains out playing Russian Roulette but his story wouldn't be complete without the finger-print episode.

I saw him one day wondering round in the corridor outside my office, a newspaper tucked under an arm. I asked if I could help. No, he was looking for Ant, one of the D.O.s. A while later I bumped into Ant. He had a black ear.

'Have you seen Taffy?' I asked, wondering vaguely about the ear.

'Yes. He's looking for you.'

'No. He's look…' The thought of Taffy let loose and bent on devilment in the offices… 'Ant,' I said. 'Why is your ear black?'

On my way downstairs I met Reg, the accountant.

'Reg,' I said. 'Why is your ear black?'

Went across to the Ops. Room.

It was like a plague. An invasion. Something out of Wyndham. Black ears everywhere, people sniggering behind sun-hats, unaware that they too had been infiltrated, colonised. Derek came up to me. Was it Derek?

'Rob. Could you spare a mom...'

'Derek. Why is your ear black?'

'Why is yours?' Indignant.

Rushed to the washrooms. Mike already there, scrubbing furiously. Scrubbed. No effect. It, whatever 'it' was, refused to budge. Taffy.

Take a tube of fingerprint ink, smear it over the ear-piece of all the telephones, go to Andrew on the switchboard, and bribe him to ring up all the staff. Voila. Black ears. The ear, being externally an un-sensitive organ, feels nothing.

I got into my car one day and as I put my hand on the steering wheel did detect, the palm being sensitive, a stickiness, a viscous mucosity. Got out, went to the washroom, scrubbed, returned with a wet cloth, cleaned the steering wheel. Put the car into reverse. Got out, went to the washroom, scrubbed, returned with a wet cloth. He'd done the gear-knob as well. So the message went out - if you see Taffy hanging round the offices with a newspaper under his arm, kick him out. He's got the plague.

CHAPTER 8

CORPORAL TYASI

C orporal Tyasi was a District Assistant. He was also the transport officer and therefore the P.D.O.'s right-hand man. He had an office which served as a transit depot for spare parts and a thousand other odds and sods, and on one wall hung a large board. On the board were written the registration numbers of all the vehicles, their condition (running or clapped), their present location and the drivers' names. So if an escort were needed, by, say, Lands Inspectorate, Derek went to Jim, the P.D.O., and Jim took him to Tyasi who, by looking at his board, could see what vehicles and what drivers were available. Derek could then go up to his caravan, amuse himself with a cup of tea, and leave ten minutes later with an escort of some fifteenish D.S.A.s.

Escorts were required at least four or five times a day and Tyasi provided an essential service efficiently. Sometimes an escort wasn't available and irate personnel from Salisbury who arrived without warning us would return home frustrated and tell a reclining world, a world like all worlds fast declining, what wankers were they that held firm on its brutal peripheries. For civilisation is always under pressure and when it collapses it goes first in the centre like a sunken cake.

Corporal Tyasi couldn't keep his cock in his pocket.

Whenever one had a disciplinary problem at a P.V. one sent either a sergeant or a corporal out there to sort it, one hoped, out.

'Sergeant,' you say. 'I want you to go out to P.V.37 for a week.'

Sergeant stares at the wall behind your right shoulder like the good little soldier he is while concern, like an encroaching shadow, spreads across his thoughtful, black features. Concern? But sergeant has served with, say, the King's African Rifles, has probably been decorated, and war is old hat. He's not bothered by the thought of danger; he has his mind on Corporal Tiyasi and his wife's possible infidelity.

Tyasi was a tall, handsome fellow, one must assume from the bedlam summoned forth by his presence amongst the ladies, a man in whose ordinary frame dwelt merry hell on wheels. When I think of Tyasi now, I see his unmoving features as he gazes over my shoulder at attention and I see the devil creating mayhem in the playground he refers to as his mind. But I can remember Tyasi only ever expressing his devilment through one medium. His cock.

There was a D.O. before my arrival who, being a tit, once mistook the devil in Tyasi's eyes for defiance, impudence if you like, and in a fit of pique he drew his 9mm pistol and fired shots between Tyasi's feet. Tyasi, I'm told, didn't move an inch, but because the devil had vanished temporarily and gone to play elsewhere the D.O. walked away satisfied. He'd shown that wog who the white man was round here.

Not knowing anything, tit minor thought he had scared Tyasi. Well, he had, but not for obvious reasons. What had driven the devil out was not fear of a bullet per se but the fear of having his pudenda pendicularia tripendentibus removed by a ricochet. For without these Tyasi's life was but a penance sent before the grave to taunt him, haunt him. To this day I don't know what it was Tyasi had, but, whatever it was, the women couldn't wait for it.

If I had invented a cheap and effective chastity belt in Darwin, Tyasi and I could have retired on the proceeds, but one never thinks of these things at the time.

How many times have I had Tyasi in my office, his eyes black and swollen, his lips puffed out like a tube through a tyre-hole, while an indignant comrade-at-arms laid the same charge. The devilment, one noticed, had temporarily disappeared but only because he'd run out of steam, and one knew with absolute certainty that beneath the chastised, pulverised exterior he was defiantly building up another head for the evening.

'Yes, Sgt?' you ask, knowing full well.

'Sir. Cpl. Tyasi loves my wife.'

Or -

'Sir. Cpl. Tyasi was with my wife last night.'

Or -

'Sir. My wife loves Cpl. Tyasi.'

The charge came across in a dozen ways but never was the essence of the relationship – that they were screwing – explicitised. (A new one for the Americans if they don't already have it.)

What to do? Have him transferred? He would be the same problem wherever. Fire him? Too good a man. If one sent him to a P.V. he'd be lolling about like an eastern potentate, peasant ladies draped all over his couch. Did one perhaps drive him into a remote part of the bush, wish him well, and abandon him? Not possible. There were terrorists out there with lusty aides-de-camp, and we'd merely be burdening others with a problem that rightfully was ours.

Electric eels in the sea and educated fleas might well do it but none of them lived in Darwin and were none therefore of my concern, but Tyasi did concern me and not only did he do it he did it all the time and unlike electric eels and educated fleas who have a right to do it, he had no right to do it where he was doing it.

'Tyasi.'

'Sir.'

'What do we do with you?'

'Don't know, sir.'

'Look, Tyasi. Just for one week, please, keep your cock to yourself. O.K.?'

'Yes, sir.'

Which gave us all time to think. If, that is, he kept his promise.

We sent him to Rob, the D.O. at Dotito P.S.O., and hoped he would evaporate with frustration never to re-appear.

One minor problem was that, at Dotito, there were two Women Advisers. In peace time these ladies went about the Tribal Areas in pretty, green-striped dresses and taught African women the ways of nutrition and home economics – how to sew, knit, cook, make ends meet, have fewer children, stay single, avoid VD. Each month they brought their reports in and met with the D.C. who tried to sort out whatever problems they might have. During the war many of these brave, hard-working, caring ladies were accused of being sell-outs by the Freedom Fighters and were raped and killed. So if they wanted to continue their work we put them into P.S.O.s, and when P.V.s went in they moved in with the people and continued their work there.

Rob was known by those who knew him as 'the General', because of his efficiency, the neatness of his appearance, the respect he commanded of his men, his knowledge of the war and his courage. When Tyasi arrived at Dotito, Rob, feeling protective of his Women Advisers, set about curtailing (curt tail) Tyasi's carnal aspirations, employing what I would call mild forms of constraint. He sent him, for instance, on long daily patrols in the bush, had him shadowed by the sergeant during the evening, handcuffed to a bed-leg during the night, locked the women in their bedrooms and hid the key. Normal precautionary procedures. It wasn't however at night that Tyasi got to them. It was on his long patrols in the bush, at meeting places arranged by third parties. Unfortunately for Tyasi, jealous rivalry gave him away and Rob became a smidgeon, dare I say a weeny bit, peeved.

The next two days and nights Tyasi spent handcuffed to the flagpole where he was fed and watered and released only to relieve himself.

It didn't deter him though, and no sooner was he free than he was cavorting and laying about him once more. The women quite simply loved the beast. Drastic measures. Rob called the women to his office and gave them a month's notice. Having fun with Cpl. Tyasi was one thing, losing their jobs another. So that the month went smoothly by with no more jiggery pokery, and, though Rob reinstated the women, the month after that and thereafter. Tyasi was jigging and poking elsewhere to be sure, but the Intaf boat no longer rocked to the rhythm of his performances.

And in Darwin men went cheerfully on duty into the bush without getting themselves bewitched by local doctors, falling grievously sick, and having to return by the next truck back.

CHAPTER 9

I.A.N.S.

Each year we received an intake of Internal Affairs National Servicemen. They were regular members of Intaf who did their national service on war stations, and were the same sort of slop as other N.S. but with the 'big deal' exorcised. And whereas Intaf N.S. wore khaki uniform on duty other N.S. went into the BUSH wearing CAMOUFLAGE.

One benefit of the Rhodesian war was that people learnt to spell camouflage. People learnt to spell camouflage who had difficulties with their own names. And have you noticed something about camouflage? Take Joe Tit from the corner of the bar where he's been fainting at the sight of cockroaches, put a camouflage uniform on him, and he becomes Joe Beef. Then put big, heavy boots on him and he becomes a pain in the arse. We slotted our N.S. in where we could. Some were useful citizens; some put their trousers on backwards.

When they first arrived, they being anonymous newcomers and all, they were oft subjected to soft-bellied abuse, but once they had settled in – got themselves shot at, blown up – and so long as they went about their business in the same disorderly fashion as the rest of us, they received the hard-nosed abuse we reserved for one another. Which was nice.

For instance. One intake of I.A.N.S. were given on their arrival in Darwin uncontrawhatsitable instructions by Ant to report to the Changamire that evening at 5:30pm. Prompt. The D.C., they were told, would call in at the Changamire at 5:45pm for a quick beer on his way to J.O.C. – which was true – and would want to greet the new I.A.N.S. briefly on his way through, which was horse-shit.

Jim the P.D.O. meanwhile had been home and tarted himself up. Jim was a Scotsman in his mid-thirties and an ex-Brit. Army M.P. though you wouldn't think it. My eight-year-old son used to beat him up as a matter of course - Ah, there's Jim. Wallop.

Jim was bald but instead of accepting the fact like a gentleman, used to camouflage – that word again – the vacant area by sweeping a handful of wispy strands across it. In the time I knew him he tried everything known to medical science to cure him of his affliction – whale sweat, snail hair – but nothing worked. The follicles were finished, I kept telling him.

Just before 5:30 we made our way to the Changers and had just started in on our first beers when the I.A.N.S arrived. They were told to enter, sit against the wall and wait while we, having our backs to them as we sat at the bar, got on with local small talk. Jim, who had been craning his scrawny neck round the corner somewhere, now entered, hands clasped casually behind his back.

'Good evening, gentlemen,' says he, smiling paternally at everything. In a blur of movement we leap from our stools and honour Jim with a flurry of good evening sirs. The I.A.N.S. do likewise.

Turning to them, Jim comes out with something resembling,

'Ah. Now you'll be the new chaps.'

'Yes sir, sir, sir…'

'Good show, good show. Welcome aboard.' And he shakes their silly hands. We look dead solemn while really fighting back the mirth that rocks like jelly in our stomachs. 'Sit down then, chaps,' Jim nods. 'You'll be doing enough standing in the months ahead, eh?' and he laughs the zealous laugh of woollen-brained, brave authority. The little twerps laugh with him and we all sit down.

Geordie hands Jim a beer (Geordie hated bar duty) and Jim, coming over serious, goes across to Mike and Ant. He asks, all looming, fatherly concern,

'You chaps OK?'

'Fine sir,' says they, solemn. 'Thank you sir.'

'Good. Good. Nasty that one today. Geordie, how's the Land Rover?'

'Had a quick look like. Don't seem too badly fucked.'

'Many bullet holes?'

'Erm, counted about a dozen I suppose, but I were busy like yer know.'

'Dozen eh?' says Jim, thinking, nodding. Then to Ant and Mike, 'Lucky to get out chaps. We'll have no vehicles at this rate, eh?' We all smile bravely. Jolly good joke, what?

I saw something resembling thought cross Yarra's gormless Aussie gob and as he prepared to open it I went swiftly across to him and whisper-coughed into his ear. Jim continued, looking philosophical,

'Well. Suppose we get used to it, eh? All in a day's work.'

It was like being on the set of an early war film. We all mutter something appropriately brave and in walks the D.C. The boss.

Now when you've spent the whole day getting up and down for the boss it is no longer necessary to get up for him when you're in the pub having a drink. He didn't expect it. So when he walked in we, like naval officers toasting the Queen, remained seated. Likewise I.A.N.S.

'Good evening, gentlemen,' says the boss.

'Evening, sir,' we all reply.

He noticed the I.A.N.S. sitting nonchalantly drinking cokes. Stared at them, incredulous. Then, getting his bearings and sucking in enough air to fill a dinghy – this was going to be a rough trip – he began. The boss's language, even when he was an itsy-bit peeved, was a lesson in scholarship. And that evening he was as mad as a rattlesnake with one tail in a bear trap.

'Don't you snot-gobbling little fuck-pigs know enough to stand up when the D.C. enters?'

They raced to their feet, dropping coke bottles everywhere on the way up, and rattled to attention, staring, bewildered, eyes riveted on the glasses behind Geordie's head. Then he really began.

His watch, telling him 5:55, pulled him up just as he was into gear and with a curt, 'My office. Tomorrow. 5 a.m,' he left.

We were in the devil of a state and when the boss left we fell about like girls in a gym class.

A few weeks later one of them would be lying in hospital fighting for his life, which we didn't know then, but what I couldn't understand was how they could possibly mistake Jim for a D.C. When you got your promotion interview the people on the board looked for certain qualities: brain, judgement, leadership, resilience.

They looked, in short, for quality in the corpuscles that nurture a man's nature. So tell me. How can a man with a Glaswegian accent pull it off? Hm? He can't. Everybody knows that. Except I.A.N.S.

There are some flowers whose dowdy presence we overlook, that feel the sun's warm light upon their faces only when a kind wind blows and makes the tall grass sway. Such a one was 'Squeaky', so called because his voice was half croak, half song. He spoke with a catch in his voice as if one ball had dropped and one hadn't, so that his vocal chords were unsure of their instructions. And he was a little swine.

During his first few months we tried him on every conceivable sort of job, all without a whiff of success, and when as a last resort we stuck him in a P.V. he was hauled back within days on a charge of attempted murder. *Just taking pot-shots at the D.S.A.s, sir. No intention to kill, NO SIR.*

Back in Darwin we let him mope around. Staff had neither time nor inclination to try reform for long and so long as he wasn't a pest he was left much to his own devices. He started, however, stealing things - something he denied. Geordie, to be sure, pinched things but Geordie was honest. When Geordie went a-pinchin' it was with banners flying and trumpets blasting. It was a mission with no guarantee of return.

One day Derek came in fuming. Squeaky had broken into his caravan and stripped it of everything but the bog-roll. Derek, having firmly established the burglar's identity, set his doberman pincer on him and Squeaky retaliated with a carving knife, injuring the hound.

'Impertinent little sod,' says Derek, purple-red, heaving with emotion. Derek and swear words were such incongruous company it made me smile, but, says he, 'No, Rob. 'Tis no laughing matter. He's an impertinent, sticky-fingered little sod. And furthermore I believe police action should be taken before something really serious transpires.'

He was right of course and we hauled Squeaky in.

What Squeaky had got away with all his life was that ordinary people found it difficult to associate crime with the picture of curly-haired innocence that met their eyes, and elusively, something inside him seemed all right.

Then when puberty left him his new voice, one's heart warmed instinctively to its strange and comic pitch. Jack the Ripper was doubtless a Squeaky, which would explain why he was never detected. Indeed, whenever Squeaky spluttered forth his innocence, I – and my office was a-litter with thumbscrews, scourges, ducking-stools and a myriad other instruments of torture I kept handy for those trying days in court – why, even I had to strive not to smile. To see the little beggar for what he was.

The boss came up with an inspired idea and from that moment Squeaky was doomed.

'Give him,' says he, 'to Geordie.'

Ten minutes later Geordie's shifting spanner slipped and Squeaky knew he'd met his match. More. He discovered that he loved things mechanical, quickly learnt respect for Geordie's mysterious ways with engines, and within months was being left to do jobs alone. We breathed a sigh of relief. Squeaky stopped stealing, I think, and even Derek forgot him.

But, oh, the gods. The jealous gods.

Months later the office got a phone call. Could Squeaky please ring number so-and-so in Salisbury. Urgent. When he came in at mid-day for his mail the message was waiting in his pigeonhole.

When I.A.N.S. came to Darwin they brought with them from training depot their personal files, and these files contained personal details that, all else apart, sometimes helped us understand their attitudes, behaviour. The father, for instance, being a politician would explain why the son lied about everything and stabbed people who trusted him in the back. I had read Squeaky's and knew that he had lost his parents in a car crash at the age of twelve and been reared therefrom by an elder sister.

When by chance I went into the front office, Squeaky had just made his phone call and had his back to everyone as if sorting through the mail. He was also heaving and I thought he might be ill but when I went across to him I found that he was sobbing. I shoved him out into the corridor, into my office, closed the door and said,

'Right. What's up?'

'My si-huss, si-huss, si-huss,' but I'd guessed. I told him to sit while I rang the workshops for Geordie, himself no stranger to life's mean ways, its surreptitious kicks in the nuts the second you look the wrong way.

Geordie took him wordlessly to the mess, packed what belonged to him into a suitcase and drove him to Salisbury.

After the funeral Squeaky returned to Darwin but, unsettled, went back to depot where he spent the rest of his national service fixing their vehicles.

And a year or so later he hit the front pages. Cars were going missing in Salisbury at such a rate even the police noticed, and thirteen of them were traced to Squeaky's sticky fingers. When he was caught he admitted to all thirteen offences and, as Geordie would say, went downstairs.

But it's as I say. He was born to spend his life in shadow, which is why, when he finally came to understand cars, they undid him. Trust Squeaky though. Getting caught, I mean, at the thirteenth.

Relax, Mr. McDonald Fraser, the dirtiest soldier in the world lived in Mt. Darwin. Tony I had known years earlier on a previous station, before the war had established its malignant hold of the country, and when I first saw him in his national service uniform I was reminded of a heap of something maggots might dump on your doorstep.

I was in the Ops. Room the day his lot arrived in Darwin and unknown to me they were standing outside awaiting the D.C. When I walked out of the door there they all were, polished, bristling with newness, crackling like logfires, except, that is, for one pile of shit hiding under a hat four times too big. I felt a vague recognition, nothing serious, paused in my tracks and moved on. It couldn't be. It, it transpired, was.

As hurriedly as appearances would allow, the D.C. posted him to Marymount P.S.O. in Rushinga District. Marymount was Intaf's response to the creation of purgatory, and only people like Tony, people with a high tolerance of squalor and loud bangs and a ready wit, survived for long with faculties intact.

When he had been out there for a month or so he came into Darwin for his first staff meeting and when the D.C. asks,

'Any problems?'

Says Tony - 'The buses always arrive at Marymount after curfew. Is there anything I can do to make them comply with regulations?'

'Shoot the drivers,' says the D.C. off-hand. 'Anything else?'

'Yes,' says Tony, dead-pan. 'Can I have some more ammunition?'

Owing to his previous record with the Ministry he was eventually brought in to Darwin to take over pay-runs. Paydays went like this.

The D.S.A.s lined up ship-shape, armed, if they wished to receive their stipend, with two essential facts: one, their name, and two, their E.C. (Employment Category) number. The paymaster could insist on other details such as the fly being done up but he was usually in too much of a hurry. Many of them could never remember their number and would have it written down on a scrap of paper. They then signed the paysheet signifying that they had received their pay. A large number of them however were illiterate, good only for marking ballot papers under supervision, but we graciously accepted squiggles, bush-paintings, nose-pickings, whatever.

Tony took a liking to one of these fellows, adopted him sort of, lent him money, took him under his wing – a scruffy, battered, unlovely wing, perfect camouflage (that word) for the orphan who had now taken up residence there. I think his name was Prune (black and gave you the shits as Reg would say) Moyo. Anyway, this chap couldn't write his name and Tony, wanting him to shine like a little ray of enlightenment, gave him a piece of paper with his name, Prune Moyo, written on it in block capitals.

'Memorise it for next month's pay-day,' says Tony.

Come the great day, Prune marches proudly up to the pay desk and writes his name exactly as Tony had given it to him – Prune Moyo. He's probably a cabinet minister now, still writing his name upside down.

CHAPTER 10

REG AND JACK

When Tony was away the pay-run was done by Reg and Jack. I can see them now, struggling into an armour-plated vehicle with enough weaponry draped about them to start World War 3. Indeed, on their return, they were concealed beneath enough dust, dirt, mud, oil, blood, guts, and wild African undergrowth, to suggest that they might have won it. Let me explain.

Our 1400 odd D.S.A.s were scattered over a large area of country in some 60 P.V.s and 14 P.S.O.s. If one were lucky one went to the P.S.O. by plane (they nearly all having airstrips, some built out of funds that were headed elsewhere but somehow got themselves way-laid) then from the P.S.O. on to the P.V.s under its jurisdiction by armoured vehicle. But if the plane was busy elsewhere one did the whole exercise by road, which took a couple of weeks. And because you had with you, when you set off, some ninety thousand dollars in cash you were an obvious target for enemy attack. I have known Tony ambushed three or four times on a run and come back half his normal weight.

So when Reg and Jack went out they requisitioned the armoury and wore it about their necks.

And of course the cash had to balance to the cent, because, war or no war, the niceties of red tape had to be observed. Every two years the Green-Ink Boys, gentlemen from the Auditor General's office, parachuted out and did an audit. Every year the Red-Ink Boys (Intaf audit wallahs) drove out and did an audit. Every month the D.C. or some poor bastard delegated the job cycled from home and did an audit. And as if that were not enough we had witless sods in Head Office keeping us on our toes.

I remember vividly one of these fat-heads ringing me up about a mileage claim submitted by one of our A.O.s, Fatty Alan, who, having his eye on a farm down the road, had tried to slip a claim through for five cents too much. When the call came through I was

69

up to me neck in a meeting with military personnel and they were in a hurry to return to their respective H.Q.s.

He droned on, me saying – 'Yes, OK. Send it back and I'll sort it out.'

But all I was getting was - 'But it isn't the first time,'

and me saying - 'Yes, alright, just send it back,'

and getting – 'There was that ten cents a couple of months ago, '

and me - 'Yes, yes.' Oh Jesus. 'Just send it back.' The meeting is throttling thin air.

I'm getting the 'But you people should have picked this up' treatment.

Me - 'We're very busy. We don't have time.' *Five cents.* 'We have just lost three men in an ambush.'

'Never mind about ambushes. This five cents.'

'Russian tanks are heading for . . . '

'They can wait. This five cents.'

I later rang the P.T.C. and asked how much the phone call had cost.

'Five dollars seventy cents.'

Five dollars seventy, plus his time, plus mine. It was the same at every station in the country. We probably spent thirty thousand dollars a year chasing a couple of hundred. I was reminded of the Crimean War when, though men were dying on the ships, heaters could not be acquired from stores because the second signature required on the requisition was on the other side of the Euxine. We in Rhodesia had come a long way.

Wishing to catch a glimpse of the pandemonium recounted in fabulous, timeworn tales by scurvy, bare-foot survivors, I set out myself on a pay-run. With Reg. It was no voyage of discovery.

We were doing the first leg by plane, our immediate destination Chiswiti P.S.O. on the valley floor, beyond the Mavuradonha Hills. Russell our pilot, who was a devil in his own right, buzzed the P.S.O. (overflew it, that is, usually upside down) and dropped us at the airstrip some miles distant.

The moment the D.O. saw the plane he was expected to drop what he was doing, leap into a Land Rover, and drive with the fury of a schizophrenic wind to the airstrip where he would pick us up. *Expected.* Today however Steve, the D.O. who wore no underpants, is off playing somewhere and Reg has my breakfast heading for the escape hatches by marching up and down the airstrip, brandishing a .38 revolver and shouting -

'Come on out, you yellow bastards. Come out and fight like men.'

'Shut up,' I told him, my sins ambling up the hill for Judgement. 'They might hear you.'

The only contact we had with civilisation was the airstrip on which we stood, the air was so still and quiet I could hear the ants getting in the harvest, and there's the silly bastard shouting, 'Come on out, you yellow bastards. Come out and fight like men.'

It was half an hour before Steve who wore no underpants arrived, and when we set off for the comparative sanity of the P.S.O. Reg spent the whole journey standing up in the back of the open Land Rover and shouting,

'Come on out, you yellow . . . '

The swine was irrepressible. He was also brave which I wasn't.

When we got to the P.S.O. we had a cup of reviving tea (I could have used something less British, less stiff upper lip, less time for a quick pipe, finish our game of bowls), and when Steve had wiped the bacon grease, bread crumbs and pools of tea off the table, Reg produced his cash and pay books and pandemonium ensued.

As the men lined up (sullen and bedraggled, I thought) Reg removed the pistol from its holster, put it on the table in front of him and announced -

'Right. Anyone jumping the queue gets a bullet in the head.'

I think the D.S.A.s realised he was joking but smiled nevertheless in case he was serious. Then it began. Reg's running commentaries were legendary and people would gather for miles when he was paying out just to listen to him. He had a comment for each man, many of them memorable.

Literate or no, D.S.A.s took an inordinate time signing for their pay and this tried Reg's patience to its admittedly confined limits.

'Come on, come on,' he'd say. 'Your name ain't bloody Picasso. Just sign your name.'

Or -

'Come on, come on. You're not writing Gone with the Bastard Wind. Just sign your name.'

When Reg had finished doling out his munificence at Chiswiti, we spent the rest of the day spreading untempered bliss at P.V.s, and when we returned, the sun being well on the way to its watery haven in the western isles, Bill, the Irish Field Assistant stationed with Steve who wore no underpants, insisted we stay the night. It wasn't a bad idea, for we could then fly off at sparrow the next day and pay Mukumbura and the rest of the valley floor. And when Bill extended you his hospitality he did so with such irresistible Irish charm you were left with no choice.

Bill has a small speech impediment, the result of an ancient battle that had left him with a harelip. Sort of. If you asked him how he got it, you got a curt -

'I was talking when I should have been listening.'

The result, as I say, was a small speech problem. He used one side of his mouth for his labials but couldn't produce 'ph' sounds, 'p's coming out in their stead. Add the Irish accent and you got 'Pook off' like book with a 'p'.

So it is impossible to convey the full force of Bill's eloquence, the vehemence with which he overlaid his invitation to us to stay the night, unless I try to recapture the endearing quality of his crippled words and the persuasive cadences of the Irish brogue.

'Yers can pook off,' he said. 'D'yers hear? Pook off. Yers got no pooking pood, yers bastards, so yers can pook off.'

So we gathered our belongings from the vehicles and headed for the showers. After a day in an armoured car the dust works its way into all one's crevices and combines with the sweat to form something abrasive.

'And don't use all the pooking water, yers pooking bastards.'

But he could cook. I suppose many years of bachelorhood had taught him one cannot sustain a wayward life-style on a frustrated stomach. He produced steak, egg and chips out of a large hat, a couple of cold beers and all was just about right with the world.

Then it started - count no man happy, the old Greeks said, 'til he be dead. One moment peace and contentment, the next pandemonium in dark glasses. Everybody leapt from the table and dived around looking for things, Reg and Bill for weapons, Steve for the radio, myself for cover. Outside the night sky was ablaze with tracer bullets all aimed at my head, the air filled with the din of a dozen A.K.s and the dull thud of distant mortars. People running in several directions at once, giving conflicting orders. Except Bill. Bill was furious.

He dashed up to the wall and brandished his rifle at the dark hostile world about him.

'Yers pooking bastards,' he yelled. 'Don't yers know it's pooking dinnertime? We're having dinner, yers pooking bastards.'

He fired off a full magazine in the direction of somewhere and stormed back into the mess.

'That pooking group,' says he, foaming with anger. 'Always starts their pooking nonsense just as we're having pooking dinner.'

It was all Reg's pooking pault. Telling the yellow bastards to come on out and fight like men. And then as suddenly as it had begun, it was at an end - silence except for hushed whispers and the rustling of people groping round in the dark and finding their way back to their stations. The yellow bastards, like us, had had enough.

Reg's running commentaries, as I say, were legendary and it was a rare situation that escaped their wrath, their irony, or their intuition. We had a ninety per cent eclipse of the sun one day and as people were standing on the lawn looking at the phenomenon through smoked glasses Reg wandered outside, looked up and says -

'Typical Ian bloody Smith. Can't even keep the sun shining.'

And as it eventually turned out, he couldn't.

Dawn may herald a new day but when it sets it leaves in its wake a trail of devastated dreams, and as we used to say, oft with awesome resignation, in those daunting days of early post-independence,

'The last one to leave. Please turn off the light.'

We might well have added,

'And when the cock crows ignore it. It's not for us.'

Jack was Reg's assistant, and was responsible, when the P.V.s went in, for initial supplies of everything from generators to condoms, then, when things ran out or broke down, for resupplies of gas, paraffin, fuel and oil, spare parts and equipment, and a million and one supplemental things people believed they needed. And, like the rest of us, he also had his normal admin duties for which his employment was intended and for which he was ha-ha paid.

Now Jack had a very large, almost obese, storeroom and nobody, not even God who had a season ticket, was allowed in there. So nobody really knew how much equipment he had. Via his half-section in the R.L.I. there was an arrangement. I believe he acquired some forty odd army assets-registers plus a master register, and anyone wanting so much as a tooth pick had to sign for it. Jack then recorded its whereabouts in both the register relevant to the P.V. and in the master register.

'Got to be done properly,' and he'd trundle off with his key, arms hanging loose like a boxer's.

Before working in Darwin Jack had been with the chrome mine in Selukwe, (now known as Sherugwe after the famous Tasmanian king whose knickers turned blue in winter), and there he had bumped yet again, and I say 'yet again' because he had spent much of his life since the 39/45 war where he first met him bumping into him, into Reg.

So when Reg moved to Darwin, Jack, at Reg's request and suggestion, followed him up there. So you'd think Reg was allowed into Jack's storeroom. Nope. Jack, like all Q.M.s who have built-in squirrel syndrome, trusted no-one.

You tried pulling rank.

'Look, Jack. I have to do stock-take. So I'll need the key to the store-room. O.K?'

'It's like this,' he'd say.

When Jack said, 'It's like this,' the answer was 'no.'

'Look, Rob. It's like this.' No.

He'd give you a good reason trumped up or genuine but it was still No.

'I've got month-end returns to do,' he might say. 'Bit busy, alright?'

'What? O.K., Jack. Just give me the key.'

'It's like this,' and you gave up, went away, and re-planned your strategy.

Then a few days later you tried the 'Quick. I'm in a hurry,' routine. Rush down to Jack's office, out of breath. (You have spent a couple of minutes running up and down the corridor knowing that Jack will spot a fake.)

'Jack, sorry, Jesus,' gasp, phew. 'Have to disturb you quickly. Need a spare radio, chop, chop. Problem at Pachanza.'

He'd look up over the top of his glasses.

'What sort of problem?'

'Sorry Jack. Can't stop. Tell you later.'

'I'll get one for you.'

Follow him to the storeroom. This was it, it , it, it. In. You had just got the bridge of your nose inside the door when Jack had closed it behind him.

Then there was the 'I'm in the shit,' routine.

'Jack, look. The S.I.A.'s flying in this morning and he's bound to ask me what stores we have to hand. Mind if I check quickly?'

'Tell him to get stuffed.'

But even Jack had to go on leave, and that's where we had him.

'Enjoy yourself, Jack. See you next month.'

The boss led the charge downstairs and after a little anxiety with the key we were in. Like kids in Disneyland.

But it was no good. Awe got to us. Jack's ghost was everywhere. We became solemn and whispered to each other, having lost interest. Well, you do, because it's not what you have that sustains you in life but the promise of things to come. So leaving everything where it was, we closed the door and tiptoed away.

CHAPTER 11

PETER THE PILL

If Darwin was a punishment station Marymount P.S.O. was the condemned cell.

When Tony got there Peter was in charge. Peter hailed from Denmark (of wealthy parents) and had been sent to darkest Africa by his father. In his late twenties he was blonde and stocky, well-façaded down to a cultured accent, and a friend of Derek's. His ambition was to be Prime Minister and he had all the qualities.

He had his first beer at 5:30 in the morning to relax tense muscles. The second, half an hour later, relaxed stressed nerves; the third the spinal column and so on until he got to the hair follicles. He also took pills to speed things up, get everything relaxed good and quick, no messing about. Pills for blood pressure, lung rhythm and liver, pills for kidneys and spleen, pills for hangovers and pills to guard against them, vitamin pills, valium, pills for period pains, headaches, abdominal discomfort, pills for indigestion, constipation, diarrhoea and claustrophobia, pills red, pills blue, pills green and every hue, pills oval, pills tubular, pills round, pills square, pills in bottles, pills in packets, pills in boxes, pills to swallow, pills insert, pills, pills, pills.

If he stayed with you overnight he covered the breakfast table with so many boxes, bottles and packets of pills it looked like New York from a helicopter. There was no room for food. You had that on your lap.

He was also, amazingly, a fitness fanatic. Every morning, after a couple of beers and a dozen pills, he would man a pack and run himself flat out for five or six kilometres. How he stayed alive God only knows, unless the walls of his heart were made of high-tensile protein or something. Peter wasn't happy at Marymount. He jittered and fidgeted and skipped about like potassium in water. But who didn't? You couldn't hear an egg fry for landmines, ambushes, mortar bombs, and Tony snoring. Only people with half a wit could stand it for long, and that half quickly went mad.

But how to get a re-posting? Ah.

Peter, it was common knowledge, was a formidable player of tennis and had his brain been under orders from any other quarter than artificial stimulants, he might well have been good enough to play for his country. There were no tennis courts at Marymount, (I doubt if there were even lavatories), and Peter complained of this architectural oversight to the D.C. He, wishing to encourage Peter in anything that couldn't be had at bar or pharmacy, transferred him to Karanda P.S.O. which had a couple of very good tennis courts. There was also less enemy activity there but that is by the by.

It was while he was at Karanda that we first got to know and understand Peter, and once you got to be known and understood at Darwin your every weakness was ruthlessly exposed and you went about naked. So what follows is a sort of literary cart - a cart-load of observations produced as evidence - preceding the horse discovered to be Peter's inner soul. Something like that.

Shambles.

Peter couldn't, was unable, to find things. Things eluded him. If things knew Peter was on the war-path they would scamper away and hide, only to emerge when someone else came looking. And the someone else, barring public holidays and times of illness, was Dixon, his servant, without whose loyal assistance I doubt Peter could have found the bath.

'Dress me Dixon,' he would say when the hangover was excessively bad.

He made a Cabinet Meeting look as though it knew what it was doing, and a minor, though an irritating, symptom of his disorganised state of mind (Disorganised? It was under siege. Anarchy ruled in there.) was the way he would bounce cheques. There was no intention to rob or cheat or mislead, let us establish that, just that he simply never knew how much he had in the bank, and the reason for that was that Dixon, never having had a bank account, didn't understand the mysteries of cheque stubs. Dixon did everything else.

In the course of time Peter ran out of people and places that would cash his cheques, and there being no bank in Darwin had to start relying on transients for cash. He had bounced cheques with Intaf, the Post Office, the Changamire Arms and every other pub, the club, the shops, the D.C., the D.O.s, the R.L.I., the R.A.F., the Police, his corporals at Karanda, Tony, me. Tony still has, many years later, one of Peter's cheques.

So he would walk up to a perfect stranger in the club and being an affable, likeable, plausible sort of fellow say -

'Look, I say. If you'd care to cash me a cheque for ten dollars I could buy you a drink.'

Fine. O.K.

And ten minutes later he'd be looking for someone else. The people that gathered about him on pay day formed a picture not unlike that of ants round a beetle carcass. Though they did stop short at removing his arms and legs and carting them off to be eaten.

One could learn a great deal about a D.O. from the way he looked after his home in the bush. For that is what the P.S.O. was to those who wished it so. Some, like Rob at Dotito, kept them neat as pins, painted, scrubbed, polished, some, like Peter at Karanda, like doss-downs.

Sometimes the D.C. and I paid unannounced calls on the D.O.s which denied them the time to tidy up and get their work up to date. We paid one of these calls one morning on Peter.

The grounds as we arrived were covered in a carpet of dirty underwear, empty milk-cartons, beer cans, baked bean tins, poultry carcasses, potato peelings. It looked as if several days' filth had been gathered together by someone inside the barracks and hurled wholesale outside. Inside, it looked like the aftermath of a violent domestic quarrel. Mouldering food and candle fat had been granted squatter status by Peter wherever he could find them a surface - fridge, stove, table, desk, and floor. Greasy pans, pots, plates, cutlery cluttered the sink, run-off, bedstead, chairs, and flies strutted around sucking up rotten juices. The fridge wasn't working and lousy remains of meat sang Auld Lang Syne while writhing milk and fluffy-topped stew joined in the chorus. Karanda was no dulce domum, no tabernacle for the weary. Peter created of it a guest-house for vermin.

'Of course, sir,' says Peter, clearly feeling the need of something to say, 'Dixon's away at the moment and I haven't had time to clear up the breakfast things as yet.'

The D.C. went ape, and by the time he had run out of coarse things to say the sun was disappearing beyond distant, darkening hills.

Peter decided it was time for a trip overseas. He was right. This is how he got to the plane. Well, he didn't of course, not without the assistance of a few loyal friends. Dixon packed everything initially so you knew that was O.K.

He insists on stopping at the pub in Bindura on the way to Salisbury and here his suitcase falls apart. Bundle everything together and put it on the back seat of his car, pills on top. Follow him to Salisbury where it is discovered that he has lost his passport. Send someone, not Peter, back to Bindura where the pub owner hands over the passport which has been found on the floor of the bar.

In Salisbury, buy him a new suitcase and pack everything for him. See him to his hotel room, where he is sick, put him to bed. Following day -

'Where suitcase, Peter?'

'In car.'

'Where car, Peter?'

'Erm.'

Scour streets of Salisbury. Find car.

'Where plane tickets, Peter?'

'Hotel bedroom.'

Not in hotel bedroom, not in suitcase. Report loss, get replacements.

'Where traveler's cheques, Peter?'

'Erm.'

Rush to bank. Get traveler's cheques.

Take Peter to airport. Keep Peter away from bar.

WAVE GOODBYE.

When you get back to Darwin, it is you who needs a trip overseas.

Peter was last seen in Pretoria, by Reg. He bummed a bed for the night, ate all Reg's food, drank all Reg's booze, bounced a cheque, and left his plane tickets in the lounge. A trail of pills indicated that he made it to the bus stop, but thereafter all is silence.

CHAPTER 12

PATRICK

Mrs. H. (Monday's got off with a bang) was blessed with a son, Patrick, who was a Field Assistant. Patrick, unlike his mother (who was the busiest bee in the hive), was a drone. Patrick was Jim the P.D.O.'s bête noire. Patrick wore a ten-gallon hat and smoked cigars, and once you understand that you have stripped to its vital essence, made naked to your comprehension, Patrick's soul - you will understand why:

He spoke with a lazy kinda, cockney, drawl, plodded everywhere kinda lazy like, his arms loose and kinda swingin' at his sides.

He rarely did any kinda work and what he did he kinda took his time about.

He was kinda bloody useless.

And why:

Everything was 'ennit', 'wunnit', like that Dickie bird in Burgess' 'Doctor is Sick'.

'Why,' you might ask him, 'are you hanging round the office?'

'Rainin', ennit,' and he would cast a weary sardonic eye at you that said, 'Poor bastard don't know anything.'

Or -

'What are you doing today, Patrick?'

'Workin', enn I,' and the weary eye.

In my first week at Darwin I went about familiarising myself with my new station (poking my nose) and about half a mile down the road I came across a concrete slab wedged between other dwellings.

'What dat?' I asked Jim.

'Patrick's mess. The new mess.'

I didn't know Patrick then, Alas, poor Yorick, but it didn't take long.

When you got tired of phone calls, radio messages, mail and sundry problems in the office you went round in a Land Rover for an hour or so to see whether it was all worth it. Whether, that is, matters progressed. And the concrete slab had not, even after a couple of weeks, progressed. The slab was moribund. Workers stood around smoking. I looked everywhere for Patrick but found not a trace, not the merest suggestion, of him. All I got when I asked was a curtain of ignorance. A week later same thing.

I decided to drive up to Patrick's house and had got half way there when I met him strolling towards me carrying a hammer. It was 10 o'clock.

'Where are you going?' says I.

'Work, enn I,' sardonic.

Hmm, thinks I. The heavy sarc with this one.

'Look. Sorry. My fault. I was assuming that because everyone else from the P.M. down starts work between seven and eight there might be an off chance that you did the same.'

'Well I haven't just started, have I? Been home for a hammer, enn I?'

'Get in.'

He strolled round to the passenger's door, lit a cigar, inspected his feet for mud, dropped his hammer, strolled to the back of the Land Rover for a rag, cleaned the hammer, watched a flock of geese fly past, opened the door, fiddled with the lock and got in.

When we got to the slab I asked why it was moribund and he replied that he had other work to do. I told him to take his workers elsewhere and find them something to do.

If there's any truth in reincarnation, when I come back I want to be one of Patrick's workers.

The mess which Patrick found so enigmatic was a kit-form, pine-panelled affair and a short-sighted six-year-old could assemble the things. Back at the office I bumped into Jim.

'What other work,' says I, 'does Patrick do apart from the mess?'

'Nothing.'

Nothing?

Nothing.

Jim, because Patrick never completed a job, never assigned him one.

We proceed. It is a month later.

One wall standing.
The following week,
Two walls.
And after that,
Just the slab.
Patrick had assembled them wrongly.
I had another, my last, try. Patrick to the office.

I explained that I wasn't being vindictive but that in three months the slab had got as far as the slab and when did he think the slab would progress beyond a slab. When (perhaps poetry would work) would the slab germinate, and grow into something more beautiful than a slab, when would the ugly duckling become a swan.

He had other work to do. Bull shit. Not bull shit – he had to help Geordie in the workshops. I knew that if Patrick got within two feet of Geordie the shifting spanner would be brought into play. Could not things, I concluded, proceed just a mite quicker?

We move on nine months. The honeymoon has gone out of everyone's interest but when life is sombre and dark clouds form we go up to the mess to remind ourselves that there's a funny side too.

There was for instance the shower. Patrick believed that the ideal place for a shower was half way up the wall with a step underneath it to stand on. So if you wanted to get wet all over you had to squat as if having a poo-poo. When however a week or so later he had come to what, in order to accommodate the cliché, we'll call his senses, the step was removed and a hole stood (if a hole can stand) in its place. A 'U' bend had now been attached to the shower-hose lifting it to normal shower height, but in order to make room for the 'U' bend a piece of the ceiling had been hacked away. So if you wanted to get wet in the shower, if that was what you'd come to do, you now had to stand six feet away from it, because otherwise the water hurled its energy at a spot some nine inches above your head.

Then there was the sewerage disposal pipes. I wish I were making all this up.

The ground where the mess stood rose and fell all over the place and the mess itself eventually leaned in many directions, so that when the sewerage pipes seemed to travel uphill I assumed it to be an optical illusion.

Jim asked the African builder which way they traveled.

'Why, up, sir,' says he leaning suicidally against one of the walls.

'Then why do you not do something about it?' asks Jim, voice climbing.

He had tried, says he, but that's how the boss says they must be.

Aeons later Veterinary Department asked if it was O.K. to use the mess for a night.

'Sure. Of course.' And thought no more about it.

The following morning a red-faced Vet. Officer came to see us. He had used the toilet that morning and on finishing his business had swivelled from the hips to press the lever, bent down to pull up his trousers, and received, cascading all over his feet and legs, what he thought he'd just got rid of.

Bill Irish erected one of these messes at Mukumbura, complete with plumbing and lights, in one month.

Now. We were determined to finish the P.V.s this side of the twenty-first century, and knew this was only possible so long as Patrick had nothing to do with the exercise. If we were discussing P.V.s and we saw Patrick strolling over the horizon we changed the subject. Pretended we weren't there.

However.

Two P.V.s, 5a and 5b, were separated by a river, and we realised well in advance that it would have to be forded by a small crossing. At its narrowest it was little more than a stream and a small concrete affair – about a day's work – was all we had in mind. Yarra would have caked it, eaten it, in a morning so, well, whad'yer think guys? Try Patrick on it? Couldn't possibly take him more than a month. And it would get him out of the way for a while. Hip, hip, hooray.

Now I'm not saying he was unpopular, because he wasn't. It was just, well, pleasant when the blundering oaf wasn't around. Patrick was in fact a fine sportsman. On the tennis court he moved with speed and agility, and his matches against Peter were worth traveling to watch.

Jim sent him out to Nembire P.S.O. to put the crossing in. Now different people have different ways of preparing for their sojourns in the bush.

There are those who, wishing to take home-comforts with them, take a day preparing themselves. Many people, requiring but the barest necessities, take a couple of hours, while Geordie who ate, slept, and worked in the same clothes and only took an Uzi and a bottle with him, ten minutes. Some, when the D.C. was on the warpath, went straight out naked.

So Patrick, having been told on the Monday to nip out to Nembire for a couple of days, was still oafing around the office at the end of the week.

'Why aren't you at Nembire?' asks Jim.

'Getting ready, enn I.' Stupid.

Instead of staying at the P.S.O. Patrick had decided he would take the only caravan and camp on the spot.

'But,' Jim spluttering, 'the river's only five minutes from the P.S.O. You could have finished it by now.'

'Gotta try and save petrol, enn we.' Haven't you heard?

'Oh God.'

Come following Monday and Patrick is still in Darwin.

'Why aren't you in Nembire?'

'Fixing the caravan, enn I.'

'But,' splutter, foam, 'there's nothing wrong with it.'

'Gotta broken window enn it.' These office wallahs.

'Oh Jesus. Look Patrick. Just get out there and do the crossing.'

'Moving as fast as I can, enn I.'

Tuesday, Patrick. Jim.

'Why aren't you at Nembire?'

'Waitin' for gas, enn I.' And so it went on. The rest of us began monitoring Jim's health. Making sure he got plenty of exercise.

'Fancy a game of badminton, Jim?'

'No thanks,' weary, wild-eyed, bumping into things.

'C'mon. Do you good.'

Got Jack to order emergency oxygen.

Patrick took two days just to arm himself. Patrick in his socks weighed 220 lbs. Patrick armed 415 lbs. Apart from the ten-gallon hat, cigar and University of California T-shirt, there was a bandolier filled with .762 rounds, two revolvers one on each hip, two knives one on each thigh, an F.N. rifle, an Uzi, a double-barrelled shot-gun, a flick-knife, bicycle chain and razor blades in his lapels. Slung from the shoulders half a dozen full .762 magazines, ditto Uzi, an assortment of grenades, and round the waist a belt for the shot-gun cartridges. When he was ready he had to be winched into his Land Rover seat like a medieval knight and if he fell over four strong men were needed to right him. Ha, you had to have a Blasters' Licence just to shake his hand.

He finally got going. Paragraph to itself.

In the lead Patrick, pulling the caravan with his Land Rover, followed by a heavy vehicle containing twenty A.D.F. labourers and their baggage, two heavies containing materials and equipment, a trailer for tentage, a water bowser full of drinking water, and an escort of twenty D.S.A.s. People lined the streets and waved handkerchiefs. Maidens wept.

Two days later back.

'I thought,' says Jim, 'you were at Nembire.'

'Gotta get cement, enn I. Do you want me to build that crossing or not?'

'Why didn't you take it with you?'

'Didn't have enough room did I.'

Following day back again.

'Why are you back again?' Jim clutching at his chest.

'Gotta get reinforcing wire, enn I,' and then for a week there was silence.

Jim and I thought we would go and see how he was getting on. As we got to the river it was noticeable that nothing had been started. Stopped at the caravan, got out of the Land Rover. Patrick came sorta out to meet us, sorta stirring kinda lazy like a cuppa soup.

'Why haven't you started yet?'

'Gotta get settled in, enn I.' A week.

'But what have the labourers been doing?'

'They gotta settle in as well, enn they.'

'Do you know what it's costing,' asks Jim, 'having you and the men hanging round doing nothing?' Jim's trouble is, he thinks things out, tackles problems logically. To Patrick the world of logic is a dark and frightening place, a place where goblins wait to unman him.

'Ent gonna break us, is it.' says he saving petrol.

A week later. Patrick strolling round the office with a bottle of something resembling a urine sample.

'What have you got there?'

'Sand, ennit.'

'For?'

'The Ministry of Roads,' says Patrick, and his face widens to make room for a smile of supercilious conceit, 'says the river sand out there's no use for making cement.'

He'd come back for river sand. Jim came apart at the zip.

'Get back to Darwin. Just pack your stuff and get back.'

'But I haven't started yet, have I.'

Jim sent an African builder out next day with ten labourers and the day after that the crossing was finished.

The flag-pole was the last straw. Outside the office was a large lawn and a flag-pole whence fluttered the national flag. We were anticipating the annual medal parade and ball which would be attended by V.I.P.s from Salisbury, and the boss decided we needed an extra flag-pole for the Intaf flag. It would only take a day to hang up another pole, so two months before the parade was due we gave the job to, erm, Patrick.

Jim provided a flag-pole, cement for the base, and two labourers. Tomorrow two flag-poles.

Tomorrow no flag-pole.

Patrick began erecting an additional flag-pole by removing the existing one.

We watched.

Next, out come the existing cement base and we have a lawn with a gaping hole. The hole is made into a large trench by ten labourers who appear from nowhere. Then silence. We waited. So did the geckos.

Next, arrives a truck load of local rock which is dumped on the lawn. More silence. Month to go to the parade. Then a truck load of cement, three weeks to go, then iron palings, two weeks.

Now it just so happens that Patrick is due to go on leave two days before the parade and the boss, getting agitated, asked Patrick if the poles would be in place in time.

'Course they will, wunn they.'

He poured the cement, waited two days for it to dry, axed out two holes in the concrete, put in the poles. We noted that the slab (yes, another slab) was a foot below the level of the lawn. Why is that, Patrick?

'Gonna cover it with crazy paving, enn I.'

Ah. Hence the rock.

And the palings, Patrick?

'To go round the slab, enn they.'

The finished article is going to look like a war memorial. Week to go, five days to Patrick's departure. Palings go in and are painted black. Three days to go. Patrick begins the crazy paving, leaves it half done, and goes on leave. Jim finishes it with a morning to spare.

When Patrick came back from leave the boss summoned him to his office and I went along as witness. We retraced the steps down the highway of Patrick's failures, interrupted at every embarrassing mile-stone by a staccato of indignant ennits, dunnits, and wunnits and finally losing his rag the boss fired him.

Alas, we also lost the services of Patrick's busy mother but after they had left we discovered where Patrick had been all those times we lost him. Up in his attic were tin lids full of cigar stubs, bottles of empty whisky, and a shop load of cowboy books.

CHAPTER 13

RUSSELL

I was dropped off one day at Nembire P.S.O., alias Fort Misery, by the A.D.F. pilot, one Russell. So when Colin the D.O. came to pick me up at the airstrip he found me stumbling blindly into trees and empty fuel drums. Russell's flying had this effect on everyone. People with a hundred flying hours would bite and scratch, holler their heads clean away, and hold onto the tail-wing with the ferocity of demented animals, when they learnt they were flying with Russell.

A great number of aircraft flew into Nembire that day as there was, ssh, someone might be listening, an operation on, and army, air-force and police personnel could be seen getting off their planes smiling and happy, while people who had flown in with Russell were malarial grey, stared wildly at you like animals at bay, and fled blindly down ant-holes. Russell didn't seem to notice.

One day I went up to the airfield to meet Russell who was bringing auditors out from head office. He taxied the plane in, got out, and strolled across towards me oblivious of all but the songs of birds. He lit a casual cigarette, smiled in recognition, and we leaned against the Land Rover passing on small bits of news. Over his shoulder I surreptitiously watched his passengers emerge, crumpled and unsteady like a butterfly from its chrysalis, and stumble blindly round, colliding with oildrums and falling into latrines. I once took a couple of innocent police friends on a trip to Mukumbura with Russell. Little did they know as they smilingly clambered into the plane but they were about to experience a morning's worth of manic, aerobatic tom-foolery the batty bastard in the driving seat called flying.

There they were, doors locked, strapped in, no earthly means of escape, and the ignorant sods are smiling away like lambs headed for the abattoir.

Now there is something everyone in the world does when they get into a small aircraft and that is study the dials. Both fuel tanks on empty. That didn't bother me because I'd seen it all before, but when I turned round to my two police friends there was something on the way to concern, at least query, on their faces. Should they draw Russell's attention, I could see them thinking, to the fact that there was no fuel on board?

He lit a cigarette, and as we skimmed along the tops of trees – he never used the sky available to him believing life safer amongst the trees – he gazed casually out of his side window, seemingly unaware of the monstrotitanic baobab tree that loomed ahead. If we maintained our present course we would hit it smack on and roughly half way down its hideous, red trunk. On it came, inevitably and unseen by Russell, who still gazed out of the window. It didn't bother me. I'd seen it all before.

At the last, not the second last, not even the third or fourth last, but the very, very last moment Russell sighed, yawned, drew back the stick, and we glided inchfully over the top.

I caught sight of the policemen and it was clear now that they wondered what sort of maniac sat at the wheels. They knew nothing, these foolhardy adventurers, because Russell hadn't begun yet. On the way to Muckers lie the Mavuradonha Hills, and Russell now snake-winds his way through them. The trees in the ravines flash past, their branches tapping against the windows. That's OK. But what isn't OK is that as you emerge Russell hurtles into space and two seconds later you gaze at the valley floor, now a mile below, and wonder how you got there.

In the hazy purple-orange distance you now see the outlines of Chigango P.S.O. Being a mile up has my knees chattering. Wait for it.

'Would anyone like a close look at Chigango?'

And the slow-witted oafs in the back nod with enthusiasm, not knowing that when Russell's around enthusiasm is the gate-way to madness.

'Yes, yes, sure.' Gosh, what fun.

Not that it mattered. Russell had made up his mind. He, in that torture chamber, was boss. The rack was his and he had you pinioned to it.

'Erm,' I began. 'Look Russell. Erm, I am in a bit of a hurry, I'm afraid.' I was afraid alright.

'Oh,' cheerfully. 'It'll only take a couple of seconds to take a quick look.' Which is why I'm afraid.

Russell's idea of a quick look goes thus:

First drop out of the sky like a hawk onto a rabbit and level out a yard from the ground. Fly like a bullet past the earthen walls, waving to scurrying sentries on the way, gain a bit of height and go back the way you've come, with added spice lest the dish be not already hot enough, sitting on your heads. Straighten up, dive bomb the water tower, and race skywards up the face of a sheer, imaginary cliff. Level out. Russell now lights up a cigarette and offers them round. You gag quietly, fearful of shaking what is left of your head.

All I do now is pray, knowing that so long as God is everywhere the devil in the driving seat cannot harm you. Because you don't know if the fiend intends having a close look at Mukumbura before he lands. Even to this day I don't know what Chigango looks like from the air.

You proceed to Mukumbura which he overflies, entering Mozambique.

'Russell, erm.'

'Oh, sorry,' and he goes onto a wing tip in a multiple-G turn which bursts your head and causes black-outs. When you land some two minutes later Russell gets out, lights up a cigarette, and saunters off to chat with friends. When you get out you think you're under water. The only sounds you hear are inside your head and they are blurred and make no sense. You are aware via the gift of sight of shapes, of being somewhere. You stumble down latrines.

In all the time I knew Russell he only had, for all his time in the air, two accidents, both resulting from enemy fire, and on the second occasion, though bleeding half to death and the engines already dead, he got his plane and himself safely to an airstrip both, with a little patching up, re-usable.

He dropped in to see me on another station a few years later and as his passengers stumbled round he asked if I would like to take a flip round the district. Flip? Flip? You mean a quick look?

I ran from him wailing and hid in the toilet 'til he'd gone. He still flies, though I believe with more circumspection, age and a little arthritis having caught up, but you won't get me up there with him. Not for a month on the Riviera with that other Russell, Jane, you won't.

CHAPTER 14

MARRIAGE

The things we had to do. One morning, a lanky length of human despair with Eddie Cochrane hair walked into my office. The concoction known as tea in the office was sitting at the base of my stomach making me want to faint (we used to maintain that Matthias, the tea wallah, spooned the tea leaves into his socks and boiled them in an empty paraffin can), so I was in no mood for disasters. Eddie, for his real name was Ted, would be in his middle forties.

'I know this sounds stupid,' says he, shuffling his feet, 'but I want to get married.' He was as Brummie as a disused canal and worked, I learned later, for the Ministry of Roads. What he wanted was a special licence.

'When?' I asked, praying for sometime after Armageddon.

'This afternoon.' Oh shit.

To qualify for a D.C.'s special marriage licence all you needed was proof of two weeks' residence in Rhodesia, ten dollars in your pocket, a good set of nerves and a woman. The Marriage Officer had first to satisfy himself that both parties were single and over the age of consent. Only a few days earlier we had received a telex warning us of an illegal couple on the loose somewhere trying to pull a fast one – effect an illegal union. The telex provided descriptions and stations had to be on their toes.

So, having contented myself that his documents were in order, I shoved a handful of forms at him, told him to fill them in and return at 2 o'clock.

'With my fiancée?' His nerves were going already.

'If you want to get married.'

Marriages were a ball-ache.

At mid-day a couple of slaves shambled in dragging ankle-irons to sweep the floor, tidy up the squalor by dumping it next door, dust off spiders' webs, evict wasp-bees' breeding grounds and gecko droppings, and remove the notice board. The desk I tidied myself making sure to put the rude notice in one of the drawers.

My wife, Sandra, acquired a vase and flowers from the cemetery, and Daphne, the D.C.'s secretary, found the marriage file which I went through making sure the ceremony format was there. Went down to Andrew on the telephone exchange to tell him no phone calls after 2 o'clock, informed the D.C., put a suit on.

All for a bloody marriage.

Now there are those who, when the mood is serious, will tell you that marriage is a matter of consequence, irretractibility. They perceive somewhere in the concept something of a socially proper nature, a commitment of some sort. I've met a few people like that.

So when you arrive at the office at 1:45 you will find the couple already there complete with best man, close relatives, and piss-artists there only for the reception afterwards. And everybody whispers, such is the solemnity of the occasion.

I once walked into a bar in Pretoria after the South African Rugby side had lost to the All Blacks. It was like being in a primaeval swamp whose inhabitants come up only to re-charge their supply of oxygen, whisper to the barman 'Brandy and water' and disappear once more beneath its sombre surface. Whisper. It's the solemnity of the occasion.

So you smile helpfully, broadly, assuringly, at the two in the condemned cell, and say, 'OK?' being careful not to whisper yourself. 'Everyone present?'

And the bride will reply, 'We think so.'

Forget the groom. He's gone. All that remains of him is an inane grin chiseled into his face like a footprint in concrete.

The best man you know immediately. He's the smug young sod fingering his jacket pocket. He's been doing that since breakfast-time. OK.

Get them all trooped in and seated, adopt an air of confident efficiency and get down to particulars. Study the forms they've completed. This takes a minute or two and things get so solemn now you feel a degeneration of attitude and must keep a firm lid on the mirth that wells within. Laugh now and you destroy everything.

Cough rather. Anything. Try to hear what the wood-worms are saying.

'Birth Certificates?' The bride has those.

'Divorce Certificates?' The bride has those.

As Marriage Officer you may ask any questions you like, demand any document. You don't because time is precious. The threads holding the occasion together are delicate and depend on the hypnotic state of the groom. He must not be allowed to wake lest he realise his predicament.

You press on. Begin the ceremony.

The groom will watch everything you do like a moron under instruction, desperate not to cock things up. Put your pen down and he'll follow the movement. Scratch your head, the same. Move your left hand surreptitiously below the desk to scratch a ball-itch and he'll follow your hand until it disappears from sight. What you're doing doesn't register with him. His mind has gone. Close relatives weep.

When the thing's finished you ask for the ring and nine times out of eight he is trembling so badly his hands are like leaves in a hurricane. He'll be utterly incapable of co-ordinated movements and the bride will have to put the rope, erm ring round herself. There are now twelve forms to be signed, apart from the Register, and the bride will finish the lot while the master of the house is still double-handedly battling with the first.

Finally someone has to produce a ten dollar revenue stamp. The bride has that. The groom, wits, now that it's over, returning, will look around and begin to take things in like a baby beginning to focus, and he is so overcome with elation he doesn't care that his reprieve has been refused.

Ted and Anna the people getting married that day, had no best man, no relatives and no friends, and therefore no witnesses. These roles were played by Sandra and Daphne. I noticed during the ceremony that everyone's attention seemed riveted to the wall behind me. Nothing sank in and when it was over I thought, apart from Ted catching the edge of the desk with his shirt sleeve and knocking the vase and its contents all over the paper work, it had gone quite well. I hadn't hit anyone which was always a good sign.

Now in those days you'd see weapons everywhere. Walk into any office and there would be an Uzi on the desk, an F.N. in the corner, a pistol hanging from a cupboard door, and often all three and more. Some people took their weapon to the toilet with them. They became a way of life, part of the dress, and unless they were out of the ordinary, a strange make or model, you didn't notice them. When therefore I had kissed the vibrant bride and shaken Ted's clammy fist he said,

'Thanks for a nice ceremony,' and he scratched his head, 'but what are they doing here?'

He pointed behind me and there, propped against the wall, were two double-barrelled shotguns.

Ted and Anna were divorced a few years later, and Ted subsequently married an African nurse by whom he had two children. That marriage however was also doomed. They were returning to Bindura one evening when a truck careered across the road and hit their car head on. The petrol tank blew up and before Ted and Mercy could get out the blaze fused their bodies to the upholstery.

Daphne also died a couple of years ago, of cancer in Cape Town. Born in the West Indies and educated in England, she was freightflee awful, dahling. When she came to Rhodesia she met and married David, a farmer in Darwin and a former captain in the Brit. Army with whom he spent many years in India. Frartflar Puckah. He stayed at the Windsor when in town.

After Ted and Anna's wedding we opened the Changers early so that we could join them in a celebratory drink and at 4 o'clock David, who happened to be in Darwin shopping, sauntered in, his Uzi slung across his shoulder. Daphne had received a letter from their oldest daughter in Cape Town and Ted and Anna, being new to Darwin, must have wondered if they had wandered onto the stage of a bawdy, drawing-room comedy.

'And,' says Daphne, reading from her letter, 'she's sharing a flat with her boyfriend.'

'What does she say about the Cape weather?' asked David, his mind on drink.

'Fuck the weather, dahling,' says Daphne, waving the letter around as though it were a challenge to a duel. 'Didn't you hear? They're sharing a flat.'

'Yes of course I heard you, dahling,' says David, asking me for a brandy and water.

'But dahling,' says Daphne. 'They're probably screwing.'

'Of course they're screwing, dahling. That's what young people do these days.'

I introduced, belatedly I fear, David to Ted and Anna, and made explanations all round. David offered his congratulations and called for more drinks.

'I bet,' says he to Ted, 'you two have been screwing, haven't you?'

'Well,' says Ted, backing off for room. 'We, erm, have been living together for a couple of years.'

'There you are then,' and David looked at his brandy, his mind already elsewhere. We were all thoughtful for a moment.

Then says Daphne –'Oh, fuck it. Let's have another drink.'

And that was how they overcame personal disasters, ended minor tiffs, drove away boredom, filled in conversational gaps, started the day, ended it, got through it. If something were amiss in the air, bombs dropping on Darwin, you would hear between the blasts a diverting,

'Oh, fuck it. Let's have another drink.'

The whole of Darwin, security forces, farmers, the works, was in the club hall one Saturday night to watch a film show. When Daphne and David finally left the cocktail bar to take their seats there were none left. Daphne's voice carried like a laser beam through six-inch steel, and as they stood there looking for room the hall heard the following timeless commentary:

'There must be seats, fuck it, dahling.'

'Well, there aren't, fuck it.'

'Well, fuck them. Let's have another drink.'

'Internal Affairs,' I heard someone whisper.

'Oh. Well that explains it,' whispered someone else. Whispered. It's the solemnity of the occasion.

CHAPTER 15

SEDUCTION

Court cases were usually held on Fridays but no sooner had a case got underway than my patience ran out and I would find myself hurling paper-weights at both parties and reaching for the ducking-stool. So I oft delegated the chore to Mike the S.D.O. who actually, hee hee, enjoyed it. It was the lies I suppose. I've known defendants lie about their age (common), their name, their place of birth, their colour, the clothes they stood in.

There was one case however the D.C. deemed fit to foist on me and even my enviable capacity for evasion failed to avert my misery.

A young Cypriot storekeeper, a non-entity but for eyes and cheekbones, had caused a young African peasant girl to fall several storeys pregnant. The maximum fine it carried would not have crippled a beggar. Two hundred dollars I think it was and my enthusiasm for the case knew not a single bound. In these cases the father was the plaintiff, hotshot the defendant, and the girl a mere witness. We tried the same thing with murder cases but we had the devil of a job getting the corpse to come forward.

In court the girl swore on oath (what the oath meant to them I never really fathomed) that the Cypriot was the cause of her distended womb, a charge he, dodging a paperweight, utterly refuted. He'd never before today clapped eyes on the wench. The Cypriots in Darwin were people of dignity and honour and this one, I imagined, had had her between rows of dresses while a shop full of customers trampled all over them.

In a seduction case the girl's word, barring evidence to the contrary, and provided she didn't have a reputation for giving free, regular, and willing rein to proclivities of a carnal nature (if she wasn't a slut), was sufficient to nail the bastard – convict the defendant, that is. So I told the swine – defendant, I should say – to cough up and smile, but the swine was a clever swine and insisted we await the birth. He was within his rights. It was usual in a deadlock to wait until the child arrived so that a doctor might take blood samples and whatever to establish within a reasonable medical framework the father's likely identity. This usually took place when the child was six months old and some physical resemblance might have emerged. So I told the turd – defendant, sorry – to return seven months later, plaintiff and daughter likewise.

Layman that I am in such matters, even I could tell when I saw the baby that there was Mediterranean blood around. Six o'clock shadow, olive-black eyes, unquenchable appetite for twenty dollar notes.

'Look.' I told the swine. 'Cough up or.'

OK. Fair cop.

Now shopping at the Cypriot stores in Darwin scorched holes in your bank manager's stationery – eggs ten (I-a-rob myself) dollars per dozen, matches two (for-a-you) dollars per box, a dress you'd pay thirty dollars for in Salisbury would cost a hundred and twenty in Darwin. You took out a second mortgage for a pound of fillet steak. So people with transport shopped once a month in Salisbury where a dozen eggs cost eighty cents and a box of matches two.

A week later the girl's father came to see me. He told me that the defendant insisted he pay his fine in kind at his store. So, apart from the immorality of the matter, the old man, because of locally inflated prices, would receive, say, forty dollars' worth of goods.

When I called the young man in he was all rolling eyes and Mediterranean hand signals and then I hurled the paperweight at him.

'Listen you little swine,' saith I in my best BBC accent. 'You have twenty minutes. If in twenty minutes the old man doesn't have two hundred of your dollars in his hot little hand I take action.' And that, thank the subtle ways of civil justice, was that.

Our D.S.A.s had to do most of their shopping in Darwin and the Cypriot storekeepers made fortunes out of them. Their wages went nowhere as a result and a lot of them took goods on the glad and sorry. At the end of the month they could invariably not meet their debts and the office would be crawling with Cypriots demanding we dock their pay. Sorry. Not our baby. The bastards, erm, yes bastards, fleeced everybody but there was one fellow who was more than their match.

It was just about impossible in Rhodesia to get spare parts for vehicles but in Darwin they were like disused flying saucers. One of our Cypriot friends however had a garage and although it was a junk-artist's dream it had amongst the junk a lot of useful stuff. Geordie was onto this quicker than light. Donning overalls ten times too large for him with pockets sewn into them the size of sandbags, he'd walk into the garage and ask its owner if he had such and such a part. Then as he was escorted round,

'Is dis-a-da part you're a-look for?'

'No,' saith Geordie pocketing it behind the owner's back.

'Dis?'

'No,' pocketing something else.

'Dis?'

'No,' and so on.

When Geordie could carry no more weight he would shrug, pull a downcast face, say,

'Sorry, you don't have it,' and stagger out and away.

In two years Geordie must have pinched enough spare parts and scrap metal to build his own flying saucer. As he always said, if you want to pinch something just walk out the gate with it.

The Cypriot shops fronted on the main road through Darwin. There was only one, what one might call road, I suppose, and the Cypriot shops fronted on it. So a stranger driving through got the wrong impression. He saw buildings that have never heard of paint, buildings with broken, heavily-barred windows, buildings with corrugated iron roofs rusted through by decades of rain, buildings whose ribs showed through the plaster. If he ventured inside he was engulfed by dark, badly lit, uninviting interiors.

He saw frontages covered in rusting car-shells with embryonic jungles sprouting through, ancient bicycle frames providing homes for vagrant flowers and encroaching bush, dustbins overfull and spilling onto the pavement, dustbins with no bottoms leaking filth. He saw frontages thick with oil and dirt, frontages scarce visible for banana skins, orange peel, maize stalks, empty cartons, chip packets, broken boxes.

A stranger could drive on.

Complaints merely elicited a thousand Mediterranean excuses. Was this, one asked, the blood that made of the ancient world a thing so breath-taking in its beauty we marvel at its mere remains, the blood responsible for so proud and articulate a nation, a nation whose comprehension of man's soul was such that it created unsurpassable poetry, drama, sculpture. Pah. If, when naked, I meet my Maker, and He says to me as He's flicking through the Book of Punishments -

'Ah. You were a shopkeeper in Mt. Darwin,' reeling from so bitter and unjust a blow I shall fall to my knees in anguish and cry,

'No, Father. Please. Never was I. I did, I own, burn down huts and cast women and children into the wilderness, but never did I own a store in Darwin.'

CHAPTER 16

PROTECTED VILLAGES

W e knew months in advance we would be building Protected Villages. J.O.C. had been pressing for them. Ministers had learnt of the concept from ten-year-olds who read Churchill and Malaya to them. The Prime Minister told Cabinet he thought it might be, well, sort of a, you know, kind of whatsit, and what did they think. Erm.

So when the cash arrived we were ready.

An imaginative journalist – honest politician – once described the boss as the swash-buckling D.C., and if you saw him dusting off his buckler you didn't want to be around when he started to swash it. You moved about like bats in a bush-fire, trying desperately to get out of the kitchen. He summoned me one morning to his office.

The map of the district that covered the wall behind his desk he had now overlaid with a transparency, and penciled on its surface were forty-seven projected P.V. points. Although he knew the district, its geography and topography, its tribal and population densities and loyalties as well as anyone (he had produced a learned article on it years previously) he confided that at this stage the exercise was no more than a rough guide. Where the P.V.s would eventually be built only thorough research would tell. You didn't just bang them in. Things went wrong. Catastrophically. Ask Jim.

'What do you think.' says he, hopefully.

I studied briefly the patchwork of circles that were his sites. I had no idea. My head didn't contain a quarter of the data stored in his.

'How many?' says I.

'Forty seven.' He looks at the map. 'It could pan out at forty, maybe sixty.'

I began to see why he had called me in.

'You want to know how long it will take.'

'Right,' he nodded, impatience raising its awesome head.

'Jesus,' I said. I considered as long as I dared. When a bee got into the boss's bonnet you danced the same steps or left the hall. 'Six, nine months.'

'I want,' says he 'the bloody lot in, complete with people, trained guards, shit houses, wanking pits, the tout, four months from day one.'

When he wanted something he got it. Oh, he'd kill those around him in the process but he got it. It was not early May. I said,

'If the rains are on time this year, we'll need to start at the latest by the end of July. And Head Office haven't said we can have the money yet.'

'Leave that to me.'

Now I had known that details of cost would be my lot and had consequently spent much time getting costs from various firms in Salisbury and consulting Jim whose expertise in such matters was mythical. So when the boss came at me with his buckler I had some figures to parry him with.

'How much?' he asked.

'Depends on size,' says I, 'but I'd say around forty thousand each.'

'Right. Tell the A.O.s I want them.' And I left.

In the next two months members of staff who at the outset didn't know the difference between a P.V. and a basket of fruit became experts. All the information required was already on record, all staff had to do was correlate it. That's all. Locality of chiefs, headmen, kraalheads, details of tribal allegiances, population densities, nearest water supplies, roads, schools, shops, arable and grazing lands. Mike A.O. spent two months checking suitability of terrain, reliability of water supplies, measuring suitable sites, and finding alternative ones. Jim planning logistics, Jack getting quotes for materials and equipment.

So when the dust settled, around, I suppose, mid-July, we felt that on the whole, taken by and large, we were, erm, ready. Bring on the cavalry. The boss, by coincidence rather than guile I think, had been right about his prediction of forty-seven but by now they weren't all where he'd originally envisaged. There were however forty-seven. Enter Head Office. Having been fed, via the P.C.'s office, copies of all data, maps, and costs we had sweated blood, tears, toil and foul language correlating, they were now wiser than we.

'Give them,' says some tit between mouthfuls of cake, 'enough money for forty-five.'

This slice of empty-headed bureaucracy would cause everyone, no matter how distant from the centre the fringes of their involvement, nothing but confusion and embarrassment, while they who stood inside the circle smirked behind vindictive hands and waited for the sky to fall. You either put all the people in P.V.s or none.

However.

Now that he had organised everybody else the boss now set about organising himself.

A P.V. was:

1. An eight-foot fence, measuring between two and six kilometres in circumference, erected by Salwire.

2. An 'A' frame, asbestos barracks, provided by Searlcom. (Both Searlcom and Salwire made a smart quarter million bucks out of the exercise. All we got from them was pain in the abdominal orifice.)

3. An access road, built by Ministry of Roads.

4. An earthen wall round the barracks, also Ministry of Roads.

5. A water tower and tank providing water for the inmates. A Japanese engine pumped up the water from rivers, dams, wells, whatever. Installed by Ministry of Water.

6. Guards.

7. Huts and people.

A big P.V. would be one built round a school and /or shopping centre. Equipment included fridges, stoves, beds and mattresses, tables and chairs, radios, pots and pans, knives, forks, spoons, and I'm getting bored with this.

The boss got Ops. Room to concoct him a chart a hundred yards square, and on it he entered the names and numbers – one to forty seven, note – of all the P.V.s plus their radio call-signs. Each P.V. had a dozen columns to itself and into these columns went little coloured discs, each disc affixed to the chart with sticky stuff.

So if the fencing people were, say, a circular red disc, then a circular red disc against the name of a P.V. meant that fencing had moved on site. A black cross inscribed on it meant that the fence was finished. You got an instant picture of progress in the field. Clever. The chart was operated solely by the boss who proceeded to live in the Ops. Room where he was out of the way. Spot on. Except.

For a couple of weeks prior to D-day Jim and I had been in constant touch with Salisbury making sure that everyone involved would be ready. Yes, of course, they assured us. Sure we'll be ready. Just relax. So, thinks Jim and I, come morning of D-day Darwin will be a-throb: trucks of fencing materials, trucks of 'A' frames, water stands and tanks blotting out the horizon, engines, bulldozers, graders lining up miles deep and bludgeoning one another out of the way, men armed ready for battle their vehicles equipped to the gunwales with tools that would install, operate, repair. It would make the Allied Invasion look like a stage production of Oklahoma. Jim and I were standing by to escort everyone to the site of P.V. No. I in Nembire, and on our way to the office early D-day morning we were a-quiver with joyful anticipation.

Nothing. We get there and nothing. No trucks, no wire, no 'A' frames, no bulldozers, no people, nothing. Except the boss, pacing up and down like a famished lion, waiting for breakfast. Had his skin been a shade looser he would have shed it on the office steps. You could say he was mad.

It was only five o'clock and no-one got to work in Salisbury before 7:30, so we as captive audience had two and a half not-to-be-missed hours' worth of the Unabridged Oxford English Dictionary (ed. 1969).

At 7:30 we began making phone calls to find out what the hell, and what could be done about it.

Having spent weeks hustling, coaxing, tormenting people 'til they were sick of our voices, we got the following:

Searlcom: I thought we were starting tomorrow.

Salwire: We're waiting on wire.

Roads: We can't spare the bulldozers.

Water: They left at 7 o'clock this morning.

The boss was in the Ops. room, now his permanent residence, and when we told him why the hold-ups he made some phone calls of his own. His sole aim in life was to get his coloured discs on the road and at the moment they were parked in neat little rows on a sub-chart displaying their legends. When he had finished with his phone, mine became red hot. He had handed out to people in Salisbury a bit of what he normally reserved for us. Their corns I didn't doubt because I knew the feeling well, felt as if a gang of elephants had danced the tango on them.

I explained to those still inclined to listen that we were under a bit of pressure to get things going, that the pub had run out of beer, that we hadn't had sex for a week, and to cap these trying times Peter the pill had just returned from leave.

They calmed down somewhat once I had apologised for everything bar climatic conditions, and promised to get things together two days later. Went to the Ops. Room.

'Well?' says he, curt. He knew he'd planted bombs I would have to defuse.

'Wednesday,' says I.

'Wankers.' I was probably included in this, his comment on the world in general. And though on Tuesday night they began arriving they were so laden with problems we still wondered if on the morrow the circus would be ready to roll. Enter A.D.F. and Jack, alias nursemaid.

Not enough fuel. A.D.F. supplies fuel.

Grader broken down. Geordie fixes grader.

Truck with puncture and no spare. A.D.F. provides spare.

Forgotten lavatory paper. Jack finds half a roll.

The problems were legion, this but a foretaste of the myriad daily hassles we would face in the coming weeks. Around mid-day Jim and I set off, trailing our staggering column behind us, and a couple of hours later we arrive at the site of P.V. 1. Everyone starts setting up camp and you have something resembling a still from an early American gold rush.

There are trucks, tractors, bulldozers, Land Rovers, trailers, water-bowsers, tanks, fencing, 'A' frames, tents, gas stoves, paraffin fridges, pots and pans, hirelings, guards, dogs. The fair is in town. Jim and I look at each other. If this shambles installs forty-seven P.V.'s in the next four months the Persian invasion of Greece was just, hell, a matter of finding the right requisition. The boss is happy. But.

First week. Wait. First day. Searlcom's white overseer runs away and isn't seen for another two years. Get another. Picks, shovels, hammers, nails, screws, have all been left behind. We went to Jack. There are no complete sets of 'A' frames, fridges don't work, some of our guards run away during the night. And as yet the terrorists haven't moved a muscle.

Logistics demanded that roads go in ahead of fencing to provide access to sites that might be kilometres from nowhere, and fencing had to be ahead of 'A' frames ditto water to provide minimal protection. A typical conversation with Roads might be,

'When do you think you'll finish here?' Finish, that is, cutting a kilometre, say, of road through virgin bush.

'By tomorrow with luck.' Luck meant no breakdowns, no running out of fuel, no drivers deserting, no Intaf guards ditto, no terrorists blowing up equipment. No rain.

'Can you hurry it up? Fencing finished at P.V. 4. tonight and want to move in at sparrow's tomorrow.'

'Try but can't promise.'

And so it went on.

Then there was Salisbury. Good old Salisbury. Fencing forgets to re-supply, as also do 'A' frames, or trucks bringing stuff out break down or have accidents. Water tanks frequently fell victim to spontaneous driving techniques and when they came off they were instant scrap useful only as tap rooms. It was a long and grinding process but in the end we did get Salisbury to think ahead. And fuel fuel fuel fuel.

Typical conversation with Salisbury -

'Your guys ran out of fencing this morning.'

'Oh dear.' (I ask you, Oh dear.) 'Sorry about that.'

'OK. When can you re-supply?'

'Tomorrow morning without fail.'

'Look, you're holding the whole show up, damn' it.'

'We've got problems with the factory supplying us.'

'Then sort them out. We have to keep this thing moving.'

Tempers went missing. You'd get a message from a D.O.

'Those 'A' frames you sent out.'

'Yes,' dreading.

'They're in the river.'

After a week we'd finished half a P.V. and at that rate we'd be at it for two years. And yet, slowly, creases were ironed out, the show began to gain in momentum, and though problems still existed in their droves at least things moved.

The D.O.s excelled themselves. Indeed, without their efforts I hate to think where the show would be right now. P.V. 3, I should imagine. Having learnt the hard way they could put their hands to a dozen things. Fix stoves, fridges, vehicles, engines, punch-ups, the wounded, and meanwhile provide an essential liaison service.

He has to go around telling the people when to move in so that as a P.V. was finished so it filled up. Nice straight lines of people, complete with beds, pots, pans, chickens, dogs, and materials to build their new homes. Sometimes he would visit a kraalhead with instructions for him to move, only to find that he and his people had taken to the hills. He then had to flush them out and herd them in. He also had to contend with ambushes, landmines, attacks on camps, and workers disappearing almost daily in fear of their lives. Quite right too. I stayed in my office, locked the door, and posted sentries. To hell with it.

The boss's chart ticked over merrily.

As the people moved into a P.V. we had to send out D.S.A.s to protect them, twenty per P.V. The task of converting illiterate peasants into fearless killers became the lot of Ant and Barry, lucky fish, though later on the R.L.I. helped out by providing instructors. It didn't make the sausages any better but it improved the wrapping. Recruits came from all over the country and we trained roughly (approximately, that is) a hundred and fifty at a time. We had, as you might guess, problems.

We could never obtain enough uniforms, and weapons we couldn't obtain at all. Web-infested ancients in Head Office lived and had their being but they did not move. Ministerial tempers frayed and disintegrated. We would watch Ant and Barry from our windows as they put a hundred and fifty ragged peasants through weapons drill, using broomsticks, cricket bats, fencing standards and branches from trees as rifles. It looked like an animated vineyard.

So of course our recruits became a laughing stock – even the police were amused – and this irritated, like a grain of sand in an oyster's belly button. And when they got into the P.V.s they lacked basic discipline for want of the system trained soldiers require. The only wonder, I used to think, was that they didn't kill more of each other.

'Wankers,' the police would say. Punch-ups ensued.

When the R.L.I. joined us they were astounded by the conditions under which D.S.A.s were trained. Yet when they'd been with us a week or two they stopped wondering if they'd done the right thing, began enjoying the work and even took a pride in it. I think there was a screw missing.

We are now in the Changamire, for it is night-time, and Barry and I are discussing deployment with the R.L.I. Enter, uninvited, unwelcome, a brace of six-week wonders. A six-week wonder was a policeman, usually a young national serviceman, who came up for SIX WEEKS to the SHARP END where he won the war, walked off with the leading lady and ended up President of the United States. If one could measure mortal man's greatest achievements, his highest endeavours, his most thrilling triumphs, in the field of irritation, he would still stand out as the greatest pain in the history of the human arse. Arrogant, omniscient, and worst of all, omnipresent.

Enter then a couple of six-week wonders, bent on causing shit.

'We can't,' Barry is saying, 'prevent D.S.A.s in the P.V. from screwing with the female inmates.' True. And it provided us with a whole new spectrum of headaches. Husbands, punch-ups, V.D., rape, betrayal to the terrs. Endless.

'Wankers,' says Pain A.

'Who?' says R.L.I. No 1.

'D.S.A.s,' says Pain B, smiling blissfully.

'We train those wankers,' says R.L.I. No 2, and before you could lift your dress there were police feathers all over the pub.

But it made one wonder. There is the ship of state floundering, foundering, on the differences of interest and the nest-feathering ways of its captain and crew, and all we can do as passengers is row like fury in our little boats, each seeking his own sweet haven and not stopping to think who we are leaving behind or how hostile the distant shore. There is always a lesson to be learnt, but nations that learn it learn it too late.

When we heard we would only get cash for forty five P.V.s the boss, undaunted, says to me -

'We're going ahead with forty seven as planned.'

'OK,' and thought nothing of it. It would just be another fiddle.

The P.V.s in Nembire therefore numbered 1 – 5b instead of 1 – 6 and those in Dotito where there were fourteen became 1 to 9b, and 10 to 14. We had, in other words, a 5a and 5b, and a 9a and 9b, being only two altogether instead of four. Got it? Now.

As soon as war broke out in Rhodesia our head office put its thinking cap on – this was kept in the downstairs toilet – and came up with a brand-new circular the sole purpose of which was to swell existing streams of paper work into massive tidal flows. When the dark clouds of head office bureaucracy burst, places like Darwin became catchment areas of paperwork that clogged up and bogged down the waterways of progress. The servant of growth and prosperity, the wise man learns, is the shredding machine. But proceed, wandering soul.

This return had to be done monthly and was known as Circular 247, and I only remember it because its leering features haunted me at nights. So when Barry came in from Mukumbura to Darwin, it was the first, he needing to be dumped in the deep end, I thought, of his new duties.

Top copy to head office, second copy to P.C. in Bindura, and a fast copy for retention. It had to have recorded on it every detail imaginable including ammunition on hand, numbers and makes of weapons, numbers of vehicles and whether running or clapped, numbers and types of radio, numbers of vedettes, and national servicemen. It was endless. The bureaucratic questions that emanated from head office drove me monthly up the wall, across the ceiling, and out the air-vent, because, one, we lied about the real position from the outset and had to perpetuate the lies therefrom, two, people in head office had so little real work to do they were able to indulge in thick-lensed scrutiny, three, we often got things through back doors, things of which there was no official knowledge – Land Rover? Land Rover? I don't know of any Land Rover – and which one couldn't, in one's mind, always distinguish from the official, and four, things went missing – vedettes for instance would disappear with mementoes to hang on pub walls – and as we were aliens to the world of truth, we lied.

As soon as 247 went into the post I hid in cupboards, closed my eyes, plugged my ears with my index fingers and waited for the walls to rock with the blast. My phone I shunned as if the earpiece were armed with teeth.

'You had 40,672 rounds of .762 ammunition last month,' says H.O. clever dick. 'How come you only have 38,436 this month?'

The bureaucrats in head office actually believed that on the last Friday of every month, I went down to the armoury and spent the weekend counting forty-odd thousand rounds of assorted ammunition. I thought of writing to a couple of terrorist cadres (top copy to head office) asking for a ceasefire because Intaf bureaucrats were worried about the amount of ammunition we were using.

'Well, we had to fire a few off,' was my weary answer.

'That's a lot of firing practice.'

I used to wonder which planet they were phoning from. There was a war on, dammit.

'You had three oxen last month. Why four this?' These beasts were used to draw water on certain types of well.

'Natural increase.'

'Why have you got eleven Land Rovers when last month you only had ten? You haven't received another.'

You hadn't officially. Now where, you think furiously, did that other come from? Jesus. Lie.

'You're quite right.' They liked that. 'Sorry, that should read ten,' and then amend your fast copy so as not to make the same mistake the next month. Then along came the P.V.s.

So 247, wishing to keep pace with H.O.'s appetite for details, began to assume dimensions so grotesque you needed an empty field to lay it out flat. It wanted to take over, run the show, and had to be sworn at regularly to teach it its place. It demanded that details be entered into its zillion columns of P.V.s started, P.V.s finished, P.V.s populated and manned, those with fences, those with barracks, those with water, radios, furniture, expendable stores, and costs of same.

Much of this information was on the boss's chart in the Ops. Room so it was easily fiddled, sorry, brought up to date, except for 5a and 5b, and 9a and 9b, because officially only 5 and 9 existed.

Head Offfice - 'Why did 5 cost twice as much as 1 to 4?'

We've started . . .

'Very big,' which kept them busy.

'Why did 9 cost twice as much as 6 to 8?'

'Very big.'

Everyone on the staff, including D.A.s and vedettes in the Ops. Room, maintained unofficial mental notes of the a's and b's while remembering that official b's didn't exist. They were fenced and walled, equipped and inhabited, but didn't exist. They had, like a politician's conception of the people who voted for him, all the substance of reality but no being. OK. We could keep half-baked cookies in H.O. at bay with our prevarications, oscillations and vacillations (bloody pretentious words) but there was one clever devil who saw through our smoke-screens and was onto us almost from the outset. The P.C. would phone me up, ostensibly to chat about the crops, and during the conversation ask, suddenly, innocently, cunningly -

'How many P.V.s you got now, Rob?'

'Thirt...erm, eleven, sir.'

And so with the rest of the staff. Permanently on their toes, like boxers awaiting a sudden lunge. After the laying of many traps and always finding them empty, he decided to come up and see for himself.

The boss stopped me in the corridor.

'The P.C's coming tomorrow to look at the P.V.s.'

'All of them?'

'All of them.' I smiled.

'We are,' the dawn of a smile breaking across his face, 'in the shit,' and he collapsed with laughter. 'Again,' and away he went roaring his imperious head off.

If the Holy Ghost planned to visit his district, the D.C. expected one of the angels to inform him, and this courtesy he extended to his D.O.s. So Colin at Fort Misery and Rob at Dotito were duly informed of the impending shootout. Now although staff constantly bitched about the boss's daily tantrums, tantra, when an outsider threatened they rallied instinctively in fierce loyalty. The message went out. P.C.'s coming tomorrow, shit's going to fly, and a blanket of silent conspiracy, as natural as nightfall, descended out of the shadows and enveloped the little world in which we lived.

As soon as he arrived the P.C. was whisked across to the Ops. Room for a quick up-to-the-minute briefing – the chart, I noticed, had upped sticks and evaporated – and then hurried out to Nembire.

The P.C. was not in fact an enemy and we were anxious not to aggravate the man – he was only out gathering nectar and we wanted to avoid his sting. He had a broad, forgiving streak to his nature, a quality that stood us in good stead over the years, he was understanding, patient, and, not least, very gallant. He was well liked.

Accompanying the P.C. were the boss, Jim and myself. Jim came along because the boss, frankly, was short on the technicalities, so, frankly, was I, and so, frankly, was Jim but only I knew that. Anyway, being a Scot he was useful to have around when smelly substances struck the ventilator.

We picked up Colin at Nembire and went straight to P.V. 1. The P.C. poked into, at, through, over and under everything in sight and we were happy to field any questions that came bounding our individual ways. At the end of an hour he seemed quite satisfied and we moved onto P.V. 2. Same routine but with less enthusiasm – P.V.s were a bore, see one, see all. I hated the contraptions, everybody hated the contraptions. The presence of P.V. 3 was scarce acknowledged, it was so ordinary, ditto 4 and...

All that separated 5a from brother b was a small river (remember Patrick's crossing?) and about eighty yards of bush, and we had just completed our tour of the former when the P.C., despite our merry, diverting chatter as we edged him towards and, dearer to our hearts, into his vehicle, halted and lingered thoughtfully at the side of the road, his eyes riveted on the mirage that stood defiantly astride the ridge yonder side of the river.

'That then is 6,' says he harmlessly to the boss.

If the boss lied and said 'Yes' then Rob at Dotito, like the rest of us, would be doing some very nifty foot-work. Because 6 real would become 7 for the day, 7 real 8, 9a and 9b, 10 and 11 and so on. We then had to hope the P.C. would go home once he's seen 11 alias 9b because officially we only had eleven P.V.s when just round the corner from 9b were two more. OK? No-one, particularly Rob who lived out there, could keep this up for long without cocking it up, because it would be like swapping round the names of your friends and trying to remember who was now what. Especially if the P.C. hurled questions at you rapid fire. All this went rapidly through everyone's mind.

'Sorry, sir,' says the D.C. to the P.C., knowing that time, unless someone did something, was up.

'That is No. 6,' reiterates the P.C., staring quietly at the offensive object. ('Ah,' I could see him thinking, 'so that's one of them.')

The boss turned to Jim who thus far had been enjoying the show from the peanut gallery.

'Jim, that is No. 6, isn't it, or is it?' which wiped the smile off his bloody face and no mistake. The boss had flighted the ball into Jim's half of the court and it was white hot.

'Sorry, sir?' says Jim furiously thinking how he might play it.

'Is that No. 6?'

The P.C. said nothing. Just gazed into the distance while the wind blew the hair about his head. It was a hot day, the juice was pouring out of us, and the P.C. was letting us stew in it. Jim looked helplessly at me. Me bent down and plucked a spear of grass.

'Actually,' says Colin, whom we'd forgotten and was smoking quietly, 'it's a sort of extension of 5.' The P.C. turned round.

'What sort of extension?'

'Well there wasn't enough room this side of the river to accommodate all the people under their kraalheads, so we made a sort of extension.'

'Yes, yes, yes,' we all nodded. An extension. Well done, Colin.

'So,' says the P.C., 'it's in fact another P.V.'

Colin having done his stuff, the boss entered the fray, and by the time he'd finished speaking the P.C. wasn't sure whether it was a separate P.V., an extension, a Martian colony, or a pint of best bitter.

When, with Rob, we came to 9a and 9b there was no prevaricating, oscillating, vacillating.

'It's the same sort of set-up as 5a and 5b,' says the boss and that was that. The next day however I noticed there were no a's and b's on the boss's chart. It was straight 1 to 13 and we had to change 247 the following month accordingly.

And the day after Barry took 247 off my hands he came to see me.

'Rob,' he asked. 'Must I actually count ammunition on hand every month?'

'Of course,' I said. 'You don't want to lie, do you?'

'Of course not.'

'Well, then.'

CHAPTER 17

COLONEL PETER

I can only speak for the ones I knew in Darwin but there must be a mould somewhere in Sandhurst whence, after intensive training in the strange ways of austere army tradition, R.L.I. officers emerge, as like to one another as peas in their pods.

Beneath the genteel exterior lie men toughened by the system and the ways of war, men of good sense and industry, men to be relied on, not least for their wit in times of stress. They became good friends.

Peter, O.C. Browns (Army), would have been an unsocial animal but for the demands of his position, and he made no pretence of the displeasure caused by life's small, daily requirements of his time and person. He had learnt from a life spent in violent places that beneath the smiling surface of things lay great uncaring evil.

The result was an ill-humoured expression; a scowling outer layer adhered permanently to his features to warn away intrusion. Yet when he smiled it was like dawn breaking on a petrified forest, the shadows still there but given a lively, enchanting edge by light that brought them into relief and made them less of a threat. Peter it was, understanding our problems with training, organised for us R.L.I. instructors and equipment.

'Morning, Peter.'

'Morning.' Scowl.

He hated many things, or so he would scowlingly have you believe – Police were 'Ponderous Fuzz', they who tilled the land 'Snivelling Farmers' – but his favourite hatred was Intaf drums. These drums, let me tell you, had been bought by the D.O.s from Africans of varying sizes (the drums, sorry) and lived in the Changamire, and when staff came into Darwin for the monthly meetings, Changamire parties took flight with a few songs and cruised to the booming beat of primitive drums. 'Sweet Banana' I remember was the favourite, and was belted out with prime disdain for both composer and tune. Peter scowled, yes OK, but they who saw only the displeasure written in his face missed the man. For instance: I was standing with him at J.O.C. around 4 o'clock one morning, he in his underpants, listening to a contact on the radio. Intaf was assisting with casevacs. A sergeant from J.O.C. 'Hurricane' in Bindura walked in with the national sitreps – a long scroll of paper containing all the incidents of the previous day.

'How did you get here, Sgt?' asks Peter scowling.

'Flew in, sir."

'Oh,' says Peter. 'I had visions of you fighting your way through six-foot snow drifts.'

'No, sir,' says the sergeant, taking Peter at his face value and not daring to think. 'Flew in, sir.'

And again: we were sitting in J.O.C. one evening when one of Peter's majors, bedecked in recent muck and bullets, bustled into the room. The R.L.I. had been visiting a neighbouring country that day, and having forgotten to apply for visas had run into a storm of sophisticated resistance, weaponry and equipment only read about in 'Jane' and troops from beyond the curtain who were trained to use it.

'We had to get out, sir,' says Kip, the major.

'Don't worry,' says Peter. 'Don't worry. Nobody's brave.' People were aware that he hadn't finished and there was a long pause. 'Unless, of course, he's British.'

Which went down like the Titanic, oodles of ice.

So at least once a month the Changamire drums kept him awake all night. Unfortunately for him he occupied a small Intaf house, a fact of which he was mercilessly reminded, and as the house was only yards from the Changamire the noise of the drums bore down on him from close quarters and swamped his senses. He wouldn't move from the house and live elsewhere because from the verandah where he drank his nightly whisky he enjoyed an aspect of hills and bush and peace sometimes and things.

'Morning, Peter,' you'd say.

'Morning.' Scowl. 'Those fucking drums kept me awake again last night.'

'What sort of time?'

'1 o'fucking clock.'

'Really? Packed up early.'

He got no change at all. So he tried a different tack.

Peter's adjutant was Bob. He had Groucho Marx eyes, a black Groucho Marx moustache, and was known, surprisingly I suppose, as Groucho. When I went to my first J.O.C. I was baffled by the call signs, the situation prevailing, the many mechanics, and could only sit there like bemused bait. Nothing made sense, a fact I mentioned to Bob.

'No problem,' says he. 'Come round for an hour and I'll explain.' Darkness gave way to light. However.

I walked one night into the Officers' Mess for a drink and was about to order when Bob came across and asked what I would like. As we sat down says he, opening old wounds,

'Listen, arse.'

'Speak,' says I, 'snot of my favourite rag.'

'Last night, foul turd, the sweet repose of sleep came tardy to my weary soul.'

'Tut,' says I. 'Such news doth grieve me sore. How may I help?'

'The drums were noisy late last night. I don't suppose you care.'

'I'll see what I can do,' says I. 'This much to you I swear.'

I mentioned the problem to the lads.

'Tell him to get stuffed.'

'Well?' says Bob the next day.

'Get stuffed.'

Drastic action was required.

A party celebrating the death of Oliver Cromwell (we never missed an anniversary) was held one night in the Changamire and R.L.I. and R.A.F. were invited. The next day however the drums had upped and beaten it. We had our suspicions as to their whereabouts but could prove nothing, though we spent a week searching. Still nothing. Bob bore an expression of innocence as light and benign as a falling snowflake and even Peter went about smiling.

Dustbin lids weren't the same, the timbre was tinnily awry and didn't carry, and the lads moped drumlessly around. Changamire parties petered out soullessly for want of spiritual nourishment, and when a party celebrating the birth of Richard III was held, it failed. A dozen ladies with scarce a handful of morals between them arrived from Salisbury to give the Changers an exclusive but they performed nudely to a wall of indifference and left unmolested vowing never to return. Life was plain rotten.

It just so happened that Intaf had offered to help Blues (R.A.F.) build yet another pub and there was a flow of activity up to the airfield as inexorable as the flight of time. We got whisky. The night of the opening we were all invited up and when the speeches were finished a box some four feet square was hauled in, bearing the legend,

'To Intaf Darwin. Thanks for the pub. Officers and staff, Thornhill, Gwelo.'

The drums.

'Morning, Peter.'

'Morning. Those fucking drums...'

For all his efforts, one rarely noticed Peter's serious side, it greatly resembling all others, but there was one evening . . .

One evening after J.O.C. we were sitting in the Officers' Mess having drinkie poohs when turbine-charged turmoil took to the air. We had been getting messages hot, hot, hot that the terrorists intended attacking J.O.C. and this we thought was it, it, it. We listened a moment or so to distant firing and suddenly were surrounded by army personnel diving about like small fish leaping from the water when a predator's about. A lieutenant hurtled towards us, saluted upside down and says to Peter -

'This is for real, sir.'

I pelted across to the Changamire, which was a-flutter with women, and children, told them to put out the lights and do nothing 'til further notice. Derek asked if they should lie down. God knows. Yes alright. Went to the Ops. Room, said extinguish lights but stay by the radios. Back to J.O.C. to find everyone disappearing down slit trenches, some down slit trenches where moments before there had been no slit trenches. I presumed that R.L.I. had some sort of game-plan and knew what they were about but to me it looked like lemmings going for a swim.

I saw Peter running towards J.O.C. Ops. Room and, not having a rifle or owt else of a useful nature to offer, ran blindly after him. And what do we find? Pronto quietly sitting there, thumbing through a naughty magazine, quite unconcerned by the pandemonium raging round him.

'Have you got comms,' says Peter, 'with Blues?'

'About what, sir?' says he, glancing up from Playboy.

'About the firing, you fucking idiot. What do you think?'

'Oh, that,' says he, plonking. 'That's Scouts doing firing practice.'

'It's what?'

'Yes, sir. They cleared it with me at 5 o'clock.' Scouts used A.K. 47s and Pronto, having things on his mind, hadn't informed anyone.

The next few moments I spent comparing notes and I must say that though Peter's language lacked the fluency and floral nature of the D.C.'s it did not want for clarity.

The last time I saw him was in Bulawayo, about three years later. He was then brigadier, traveling round the country, the army representative on the National Election Commission. Another circus. I asked him how he was enjoying this, his new ambassadorial role.

'I just wears me Japanese smile,' says he, 'and at least I'm not kept awake all night by fucking Intaf drums.'

He was killed in England a couple of years back, in a way he might have chosen I suppose. But I wonder how he gets on with all those fucking harps.

Scowlingly, no doubt.

CHAPTER 18

JOINT OPERATIONS COMMITTEE

J.O.C. comprised six terrestrial units and began its nightly meetings punctually at 18:00 hours. The members were O.C. army, ditto R.A.F., ditto S.B., ditto Cop Uniform, D.C. Intaf, and an army adjutant to do the work. I have been on J.O.C.s in other parts of the country that the whole neighbourhood attended including the madame of the local brothel, J.O.C.s that would get under way whenever, depending on how quickly they could find tea-wallahs, members, typewriters, pipe-tobacco. J.O.C. prosecuted the war and its meetings were secret. Secret.

A sample from its secret bag of tricks.

The area about Nembire, J.O.C. decided one month, was ripe for a, indeed rotting on the branch for want of a, crying for a, High Density Operation. Now H.D.O.s were secret and were planned, when they were planned, by J.O.C. The PLAN was SECRET. What they amounted to was this.

Special Branch, or, if you like, someone dependable, has information that terrorists have assembled, gathered, in large numbers somewhere in the Tribal Area. After much secret confabulation and manoeuvring J.O.C. sends the troops in on foot because vehicles make a noise and the operation is SECRET to surround said area. It is a night-time operation so that come morning everyone is in position to move in, close in, flush out, and destroy aforementioned, hereinafter referred to as, terrorists. The air-force stands by, ready to mount rapid air strikes.

In an area where the local population is congregated in P.V.s or C.V.s (Consolidated Villages), where, in theory that is, they cannot communicate with the enemy, the H.D.O. has all the aspects of sound, military strategy. The ear sits up and listens. While the operation is in progress people who work in the area, Intaf, police, whatever (only J.O.C., remember, knows anything, H.D.O.s being secret) go about their normal daily business blithely unaware that the decks have been cleared for a shemozzle. An impression is thus conveyed to those who have eyes and ears of sleepy, ho-hum normality.

So secrecy is essential. Secret means.

If someone says to you,

'Care for a drink?' you say,

'Oh, is it? I could have sworn it was purple,' and pass merrily on your way, slapping tree-trunks, returning the resident lourie's call, knowing nothing.

You talk to nobody. This includes members of your family, colleagues, friends, the cheerful postman. It is just too easy to let slip vital snippets of information such as 'water closet'.

Only three copies of the PLAN are made. Two you burn forthwith, thus avoiding the temptation to read what is written there, and one you swallow. And no going to the toilet. Spies are everywhere.

You do not, repeat not, is everybody clear, doodle on your writing pad for fear of leaving, intertwined amidst the psychic ramblings laid bare by the tip of your pen, intricate, decipherable details of the PLAN.

What is an H.D.O? Why sir. It is a secret.

Then, for all the precautions that have been taken against leakages, the night before the plan goes into operation a farmer's wife walks into the club and magna voce says,

'I believe there's to be an H.D.O. in Nembire tomorrow.'

The African barman rolls his eyes, goes outside, and gets on the tom-toms.

I have never known, never been involved with, an H.D.O. that worked. The army closes in and where the day before there were thousands of the bastards, there is, suddenly, nothing. It's all done with wands, top-hats, and mirrors.

After a couple of days the H.D.O. wraps up. Trucks by the zillion come waddling down the road, pick up army and take them away, tents come down, are packed away in trailers, and towed off by Land Rovers, water bowsers are returned to Darwin, aeroplanes cart off V.I.P.s, the barracks are tidied up and made habitable. Peace and quiet returns. Life, for Intaf, status quoes. And the following day Colin hits a landmine. The bastards are back.

If you were a reporter, had camouflaged (that word) yourself with branches and twigs, and overheard, 'Intaf are wankers,' you would know you had gatecrashed a police palaver.

'Fuzz are wankers,' Intaf intrigue.

'Browns are wankers,' babbling Blues.

'C.I.D. are wankers,' Special Branch sabbatical.

And so on.

If however you overheard the following,

'Territorials are wankers,' you would be confused, not knowing that T.F. incompetence provided amusement whichever road it trod.

Allow me to speak for the ones I met, with whom I had concourse, whose threadbare souls, had I had time, I might well have pitied.

T.F. Officers, men like our vedettes, on a tour of six weeks' duty - in real life they would be teachers, accountants and such like:

1. Humourless.

2. Indolent.

3. Offensive.

4. Almighty. They swaggered about like prize cockatiels but knew as much about fighting a war as a dissipated radish.

5. Dissipated.

A mere thumb-sketch I know but lunch beckons.

It was not long after the P.V.s moved in that R.L.I. moved out, and, having dealt with men, I now had to contend with their emissions. Their very first morning.

Two young officers, a captain and a lieutenant, walked into my office. Here we go.

'Yes. Can I help you?'

They had come up for six weeks, would slouch around and smoke fags under trees, go back to their pubs in Salisbury and tell how, if only they'd been allowed a few more minutes and a free rein, boy-oh-boy.

'We're sick of Intaf shit.' The captain it was that spoke. Let me explain what he meant by the word 'shit'.

There had been a problem with the sewage disposal system, alias one small septic tank, for years. The system had been installed originally to cope with effluent from the Intaf house now occupied by Peter, but when the R.L.I. moved in pipes carrying a considerable extra load were linked up with it causing it to overflow. Permanently. Because one small tank could not cope, obviously, with the sudden onrush of effluent emanating from army kitchens and army toilets.

This problem fell under the jurisdiction of 'Piss and Wind Department' of Public Works but when the war moved in they moved out. Unable to get them to come back and sort it out, we decided one day to arm ourselves with picks and shovels and were bearing down nicely on the quarry when Piss and Wind appeared in flocks from nowhere and perched on the tops of telegraph poles.

'Hello, hello, hello. What do you think you're doing?' they asked, because though the smell was hideous, we weren't allowed by the Department of Public Works to fix it by digging extra effluent tanks. So when the T.F. captain says to me,

'We're sick of Intaf shit,' I knew what shit the rude little tyke was on about. It was after all army shit. I asked him nevertheless,

'What sort of shit,' says I.

'Your shit coming out below the kitchens.'

This wasn't generics talking. This was the major.

'Right,' says I. 'Go see major,' like 'Go see flog,' in Steinbeck's *Cannery Row*. On the way across I prepared a little speech.

He was sitting on a table in J.O.C. studying a wall-map of Darwin District like Hitler twirling a globe of the world. It was all his for six weeks, God help us.

'Next time you have some dirty work needs doing,' says I, foregoing introductions, 'do it yourself.' I was in a super little sweat. 'Cos if I see these ill-mannered heaps of pig-swill again I'll tear their arms out.' And I left.

It was no good though. You would get rid of one T.F. major and six weeks later he was replaced by another, exactly the same, forever studying the wall-map, hatching master-plans, plotting roads to victory.

Intaf Horse Troop had gone on a nose-poke in the bush and got itself into one of its frequent, piquant pickles caught in a shallow drift and pinned down by heavy fire.

'Bloody Horse Troop,' thinks I, as I go across to J.O.C., 'farting about in the bush when people are trying to work.'

I stopped briefly to chat to Pronto, a creature slightly higher on the evolutionary ladder than his palaeozoic pals, and listened to Ken (D.O., I.C. Horse Troop) on the radio, hollering on about reinforcements or some such drivel. When I walked into J.O.C. the Great Leader was staring at the wall-map (surprise), his chin cupped in one hand, his elbow in the other, as though his thought had become substance and could be weighed.

'Ah,' says he. 'Morning. Could you come here a minute.' I think momentarily on Ken and wonder how long his ammo and food will last. 'I want you chaps,' he points his stick at the map, 'to keep out of there.' 'There' is guess where? Ken.

'I've got some guys,' says he, 'in there. Snooping around.'

They were always snooping around, meaning sitting on their backsides under trees, chewing grass stems, sticking lighted fag-ends down ant holes.

'I want the Gooks (Vietnam had become a cult) to think it's nice and quiet in there.' They talked like that. 'Let things gel.' Gel? I still get visions of bears licking honey off their paws. 'Wait for them to put their heads in the noose.'

'Hm,' says I, bubbling with indifference. 'I've got Horse Troop in there right at this moment. Right there, right now.'

'Well, could you get them out?'

'That's your job,' says I. 'Look. God knows why you haven't been told, but Horse Troop is under fire right there, right now. Reckon you could send army in?' When I left he was spewing volcanic ash all over Pronto.

And on another occasion . . .

Chesa was an African Purchase Area. It consisted of farms owned by Africans and was administered from the D.C.'s office. The Chesa road erupted daily to the blast of mines and one particular hundred-yard stretch I seem to remember had more craters in it than a syphilitic nose. Only people who were terminally ill or round the twist used it with equanimity.

In its R.L.I. days J.O.C. had lit up with a rare idea. Terrorists were giving farmers mines with instructions that they plant them outside their farms. J.O.C. therefore made the farmers responsible for their own roads and threatened them with hell on earth if mines made noises on them. So the farmers, caught like nuts in a cracker and knowing that the ters would give them real hell, a bullet in the head, if they didn't plant the mines, planted them next door, or better still outside the farm of someone they didn't like. So. A mine goes up, you haul the farmer in, give him what you think he thinks is hell on earth, and discover he hasn't been on his farm for a month. He's been in Salisbury. J.O.C. gave it up.

Enter T. we know it all F.

A patrol of theirs hits a mine in the Chesa road and the major, foregoing recourse to people who might help, orders his merry band to destroy the farm. Burn it down. This they do, lock, stock and barrel.

The farmer's brother hears about it, comes up to Darwin from Salisbury, asks what the hell. He is a Sergeant in the Rhodesian African Rifles, and the terrorists, knowing this, have had the mine deliberately laid outside his farm hoping that security forces would come and burn it down.

But it's as I say. T.F. incompetence provided amusement whichever road it trod. Even the ters got fun out of it.

CHAPTER 19

FAREWELL

Golf India, alias Grinning Idiot, real name Mac, was a Field Assistant, and when the Darwin crowd began to disperse and head elsewhere, G.I. was one of the first to go. Mac was unable in the main to keep his nose more than a couple of centimetres out of the you know what. And this was, I think, due to the fact that things waited for him to come along before deciding to happen. Perhaps because they mistook his ginger-blonde hair, his ill-shaven, scruffy appearance, his low but honest nature and the way chaos followed him around, for Australian,

So when, the afternoon of his farewell, he came into my office with his face bust open and his front teeth loose and broken, I knew that some thing or other had happened.

'Hell, Mac,' says I. 'What happened?'

What happened was, he was down at the workshops starting up a cement mixer, one small job before he finally knocked off, and the handle, realising it was Mac standing there, upped and kicked him in the face. I told him to go to the army doctor and have it examined.

'Yeph. O.Hey.'

But not Mac. Oh no. He goes instead, much better idea, to the Changamire and gets Bill Irish, who is on bar duty, to state his opinion. Bill, after a cursory examination, diagnoses broken jaw and prescribes double brandies, taken with or without food. And in thus-wise did G.I. begin the party that would bid him farewell.

He was, as I say, low but honest. However, don't get me wrong. He wasn't low after the manner of politicians and journalists - his thoughts and deeds were inspired by passion not ambition. So he would never, for instance, have handed good people over to corruption, debasement and decay, but he would pinch your beer if his need outdistanced yours.

By the time people began to arrive, about sixish, say - wives, children, assorted girl-friends - Mac's jaw was pickled in brandy and created noises reminiscent of John Hurt's Elephant Man. The speech he delivered was scarce legible and all I remember of it is some story involving the D.C., which Mac in his depleted mental state found pulsatingly funny. It goes thus.

Mac put up a building at Dotito P.S.O. and when the D.C. went out to inspect it he remarked that the roof wasn't level. Mac's reply was -

'*No sir. The roof's level. It's the floor that isn't level.*'

Now it came to pass that, to see Mac off, a great multitude had gathered, and of the multitude they that found the story worthy of mirth - even lizards out rubbernecking headed quietly for the exits - were but two.

One, Mac himself who, on reaching the end of his story, collapsed to the floor in a heap of merriment and promptly passed out. And two, Rob, who being at that time D.O. at Dotito, had witnessed the incident.

Now Rob had his own way of doing things. After three beers he would suddenly, curiously, rend the air with his laughter, his face flushed with the pleasure of a private thought. Ah, you think. Pissed. I was never sure with Rob, and for a long time thought him dull-witted, that his efficient manner was merely the outcome of his thorough nature.

Tell a joke, for instance, and while all others are picking themselves painfully off the floor Rob stares blankly before him, seemingly unamused. Five minutes later, however, when others are discussing Plato's Symposium, Rob is sucked from his stool and dumped on the floor by a whirlpool of laughter. Ah you think. He's got it. But I think it was something else.

Rob related the comments of others to events in his own life. He might not find a remark of yours amusing but he could sift through a library of assorted memories and come up with an association, something that did amuse him. He watched a private show of his own which flashed on an inner screen.

Now back to the party.

When all the speeches had been made, Rob staggered to his feet on legs way past their bed-time and gave an unsolicited speech of his own. Flushed with excitement and laughter he told a story of how, one day, Mac put up a building at Dotito and when the D.C. said the roof wasn't level Mac replied -

'No sir. The roof's level. It's the floor that isn't level.'

Something like that.

Anyway, Rob found the yarn so funny he needed the arms of friends to keep him upright, and though the aspect of Rob blithely recalling Mac's story on legs that booze and rejoicing had rendered incoherent was perfectly amusing theatre, the rest of us, being bastards, maintained a poker-faced, snootily offended silence.

For Rob had been through his inner library, found something relevant to Mac's story that amused only himself, followed the plot on his inner screen and returned, as in 'This is where we came in' during a film show, to Mac's story. He wasn't just laughing at Mac's story, he was laughing at other things he didn't share.

Anyway. Believing himself in sufficient touch with his dignity to begin again, he shrugged off the arms of friends, gathered his forces for another onslaught, and told a story of how one day Mac put up a building at Dotito and when the D.C. said the roof wasn't level Mac replied -

'No sir. The roof's level. It's the floor that isn't level.'

The men, having sated their thirst for Rob's spiritual blood, now leave the women to it and cruelly drift off into the bar. A small commotion draws them outside. Ant, who has been in a landmine at Kaitano P.S.O. in the morning, has arrived from hospital, his scalp stitched tightly together like a rugby ball, is getting the gears - Rhodesia-speak for having the piss taken. It wasn't the landmine that blew you away. It was the pitiless badinage when you got back.

'Ah look,' says Mike A.O. 'Anthony been in naughty landmine.'

'Piss off,' says Ant fighting back instinctively like a cornered snake.

'And got horrid stitches in little head,' says Jim.

'Didums go bang den?' Geordie.

'Brave little ums.' Yarra.

'Landed on heady weady.' Tony.

'Up, up, up, in a puff of smoke.' The assembled gathering.

The idea was to make you relax, calm down, see life for what it was, and by the end of it you wanted to kill someone. Gill, the D.C.'s wife, emerges from the bar exuding real sympathy.

'Are you alright, Anthony?' she says.

'Been in naughty landmine,' says someone.

'Fine, thank you,' says Ant. 'Fine. Really.'

Having the lads round him cramps his style and he doesn't dare, but privately he'd like to say,

'Not too bad thank you. Bid giddy I suppose. That sort of thing.' He might perhaps lift a trembling hand to his head, have a little faint here and there before steadying himself against a chair. But to do so openly would let the floodwaters through. As it is Gill says -

'I think you'd best come inside, Anthony, and sit down.'

'Yes, yes, yeees. Ums is poorly.'

'You have a little sit, Anty Wanty.'

They were bastards.

I happened to be in Darwin a couple of years ago on other business. Most of what I remember had either disappeared, fallen into desuetude, or decomposed but the Changamire, miraculously, still stood. Mike's creeper had gone of course, as had the fence, lawn and dartboard, (progress slays me) and when I walked inside, the door being open, so had everything else. Just the husk. And I got the feeling I get when I walk into an empty theatre. The drama is over, the players have gone. But there are memories of the performance, and as I stood there and gazed at the far corner of the bar I said to myself,

'By 7 o'clock Mike S.D.O. would be sitting right there, and he would be playing crib with Geordie.' Mike never won, poor soul.

'I was unlucky,' he would say, or 'Geordie was just plain lucky.'

Resentment, blurring the senses as it does, musters excuses as a rolling snowball gathers up debris. It harries the innocent and flags the guilty on its way.

So would Mike, his anger mounting as the evening progressed, as the clatter of frustrated play rattled the crisp dishes and stilled the conversation of others, seek out Geordie's secret conspirators. He would blame the number of holes - 60 too short, 120 too long - the heat that oppressed his concentration, respective states of inebriation, changes of government, the price of olives. But he overlooked the culprit, the reason he lost. And that was the fact that Geordie cheated.

Strategic cards surreptitiously stowed out of sight in ladies handbags, beneath beer-mats and ash-trays were merely back-up. Geordie's real strength lay in prestidigitation, never, that is, dealing from the top. Anywhere else, sure, no problem. But the top? Please. Of the top Geordie did in no wise wot.

I was many times Geordie's victim before catching on and the night I tumbled I invited him quietly outside for a breath of air. He knew what was coming of course, and once outside I gazed at the stars and sighed -

'Cheat, don't you.'

'Course I fuckin' cheat,' he protested as though I were a mere rookie as yet unversed in the complex manoeuvres of established masters.

'OK. So long as I know.'

It was never referred to again but if I eavesdropped on one of his games he would glance at me the glazed eye of conspiracy that said,

'I know you know and all that. But it's only a game after all.'

You take pity on Mike and are considering telling him when you hear – 'Steven,' in the high-pitched tones of rising indignation.

Just inside the lounge door, Steve who wore no underpants is sitting with his feet up on a side-table. Gill, who is sitting across the room, had justifiably had enough.

'Steven. Would you please put your legs down? I'm tired of looking at your ball-hairs.'

I don't know what it was about Steve, perhaps his infant, wide-eyed looks, but whenever the tribal dancing began and the shirts came off, women immediately tried to pull his shorts down. Strange women would stop him in the street and within moments have his shorts down over his buttocks. Maybe they could tell. Perhaps the message went round. Steve minus shorts equals birthday suit.

Sandra's parents came out from England and stayed with us in Darwin, and the Saturday night of the staff meeting I took them sweatingly, fingers of apprehension plucking at the hair follicles, to the Changamire. By the time we arrived, the D.O.s were already shirts off and dancing and in no time at all Sandra's mother, a woman who can detect overtones of promiscuity in a leftover cucumber sandwich, was at it. From the corner of my eye I saw her, as Steve gyrated to the pounding of the drums, rapidly flick out a hand as a hen pecks at a hard pea. Then again. It dawned on me. She was trying to pull Steve's pants down.

Glad of any excuse I wander outside where Tony and Peter the pill are going through their monthly 'I buy all the food' routine. Darwin bachelors lived in a large house on the Ridge and when staff came in from the field they piled into the bachelors' mess, no 'may I?', nothing. Just dumped their kit in the lounge, buggered off 'til two next morning, picked the pantry cleaner than the moonbeams shining outside, fell down and slept.

Occasionally, this had to be sorted out.

'I do beg your pardon,' says Peter. 'But last time I was in Darwin I bought a whole chicken.'

'Yes,' says Tony. 'And you ate it.' I don't know how Peter's gluttony never earned him an honorary degree.

'And I bought a loaf of bread.'

'Yes,' says Tony. 'And you ate it.'

'Well, then.'

'The last time you were in,' says Tony, ploughing a barren field, 'you finished off the bacon, a dozen eggs, a pound of sausage, four pints of milk, two tins of beans, half a jar of coffee. You used my soap, my toothpaste, my toothbrush, and went off wearing my shirt and underpants.'

'You can talk,' says Jim, sauntering on from the wings. 'When did you buy any food?'

'Bloody hell,' says Tony, 'I bought all the food on Thursday.' There is smoke around.

'Did you hell. I bought all the food yesterday morning.' Engines are starting to overheat and Mike A.O. decides it's time to cool things down.

'You're both talking crap because I bought all the food this morning.'

I didn't like to say anything but the weekend I stayed with them it was I who bought all the food.

Meanwhile, in the lounge, Rob is telling a story of how Mac put up a building at Dotito and when the D.C. remarked that the roof wasn't level Mac said,

'No, sir. The roof's level. It's the floor that isn't level.'

Everything passes and when around midnight people are slumped wearily about the drums and the singing and dancing have petered out, the lads, realising that, but for a few bolt-shot strangers, they are the only ones left, slowly raise themselves upright and wander outside in sombre, candle-flickering mood. It doesn't last long however.

The air was a-buzz with rumours of transfer which, if true, meant that the 'gang' would be breaking up and going to other less lethal stations. I have no idea who was behind the plan because it made sense:

1. They would be going individually to stations where they would be able to share their considerable experience and knowledge of working in a war environment. Stations that were experiencing terrorism for the first time had little idea of how to tackle it, and panic ensued, sometimes costing lives.

2. And what is more important: the gang had been together in Darwin for some four to five years and it was beginning to tell.

Let me give you an example -

Not long before Rob was killed I met him at a cricket match in Bulawayo and he confided in me that he knew, not felt or thought, but *knew* that he would be killed if he returned to Mukumbura. I told him to tell the new D.C. in Darwin that he would like to work in the office. The D.C., I told him, would understand.

'No,' was his reply. 'I have to go back.'

'Have to.' It was as if Rob received some sort of spiritual warning.

Young men who have spent several years in the bush, surrounded daily by danger, and not coming to any sort of harm, begin to think, or feel is probably a better word, that they are indestructible, and this results in the making of bad decisions, decisions that lack the sort of wisdom that saves lives. They begin to make decisions that are the result of reaction rather than thought, the wrong instincts take over and then lives may be lost, people wounded. The proof of all this was beginning to show itself in Darwin. These remarkable young men had begun to take risks which after sober thought they would not have taken. Ken, Dave, Steve, all wounded, Ant in a mine, Rob killed. And all of it much about the same time. They simply had to move on.

But first, they decide there'll be a final fling - they will go en masse to Kariba at Rhodes and Founders, a national four-day holiday, now barely a couple of months away. They have, however, a problem. A problem that will not wait. A problem known as *the boss*. The war didn't stop for holidays and there was no way he would allow more than a couple of people off at the same time. Tactics would have to be discussed.

'Look. We just go to the D.C. and brazen it out. Tell him we all need a break.' This from Jim, robbed by enthusiasm of his zest for life.

'Don't talk crap,' says Colin. 'We just go without permission and take the shit when we get back.'

The word 'shit' I realise, may not be regarded elsewhere as a creature carrying much clout but in Darwin its very mention cast dark clouds of unseemly fear. It held sway over the world of dread and the earth trembled at its coming. 'Shit' had no chance.

'We could all have relatives falling sick.' Steve who wore no underpants.

Pandemonium.

'We'll just jolly well tell the D.C. that what with everybody going on transfer we'd like a holiday together.' Peter the pillock.

Tony hits on a major snag. 'Who's going to tell him?'

Silence, broken by Mike A.O. 'Rob!' (*Me)* 'You don't mind going to the boss do you? You can explain it better than us. He'll listen to you.'

'That's right, Rob.' Geordie, falsetto. 'You just go and explain. He'll listen to you.' And, 'Will he fuck.'

'Listen,' says I. 'You'll never make it.'

'Hey,' from Andy. 'I know. What if we tell the boss we'll take his son with us?'

Tony, ploughing, 'Good idea. Who's going to tell him?'

'Rob,' says Mike desperately. 'You don't mind telling him do you?'

It was pathetic.

'You'll never make it, I tell you,' says I.

But they did.

Come Monday morning Jim goes to the boss's office.

'Excuse me, sir. I know it's a long way off and all that but would you mind if I took off Rhodes and Founders this year?' Note careful use of subjunctives.

'OK,' says the boss, his mind on higher places. Jim poked his head round my door and stuck up a thumb. At the top of my desk calendar I wrote,

1. Jim.

A few days later Ant finds the boss in fearfully good humour and as they laugh and joke,

'By the ha-ha way, sir. Do you mind if I ha-ha take off Rhodes and ha-ha Founders this year?'

'No. Go a-ha-ha-head.' Ant comes into my office.

'Boss says I can go.'

2. Ant.

The following week Colin tells the boss he's promised to be home for Rhodes and Founders. Was it OK?

'Sure.'

3. Colin

Peter, a few days later, finds a relative in South Africa.

4. Peter.

The boss rarely gave minutiae much thought and furthermore he didn't have the head start I had of knowing what the little sods were up to. Over the next week or so they got their permission to take off Rhodes and Founders and as the day approached the air in certain offices shook with attacks of the jitters. They decided that on the day itself they would leave well before dawn so as not to be around when the boss discovered the plot.

Wise, I thought.

But being what they were, they got themselves celebratorially paralytic the night before, and what with hangovers and trying to find Peter's socks and underpants it was 7 o'clock before they began gathering at the office. And by then the boss was there.

We had a dog in those days, a black labrador called Fred. Fred wasn't allowed near the table at meal times because he would fix the food with an unmoving eye and drool like a waterfall. So he would sidle up unseen and pretend he wasn't there. If you looked suddenly in his direction he would look sharply elsewhere and whistle as though food were the last thing on his mind. Food? Is there food? Oh, I'm just here for the company.

The lads that morning put me much in mind of him. They clearly wished they were invisible, and as they sidled up to their respective cars they gazed about them as though cars were the last thing on their minds. Going away? No, not at all. Just strolling by. Now how did that suitcase get in there? Really, these suitcases, do what they want these days.

'Where are you going, James?' says the boss.

'Erm, Kariba, erm, sir.' Cough.

'I don't remember giving permission.'

'Yes sir. A couple of, erm, months (throat clear) ago.' Rob Dotito is with him.

'You said I could go last, erm . . . , sir.' The atmosphere is beginning to ripple, oh, so slightly, like a light breeze in the trees.

'But I didn't say you could go,' pointing at Steve who would shortly need underpants.

'Er-yes sir. Two weeks ag-erm.'

'And where,' says the boss pointing at Andy, 'is that little sod going?' The gale is on its way.

'Kariba, sir,' says Andy bracing himself for the blast.

'Hey. What the bloody hell? If you all think . . .'

He sees more of them pitching up. Ant, John, Mike, Fatty, all bearing luggage.

'And where the fucking hell do you think you're off to?'

You could see them wishing they'd got off to that early start. As it was, they stood about as fearful as doves before a storm not daring to move. Success seemed to have fled from them just as it was in the net. The boss pointed an articulate finger at Tony and Mike.

'Rob,' he looked at me seeking straws of reassurance. 'I didn't say those two snot-gobblers could go.'

'Yes, sir.'

'When?' his voice leaping an octave in disbelief.

'Sir. I wrote down all their names. As soon as you gave permission I wrote their names down.'

He knew he'd been taken. He knew it had been carefully planned, that his trust had been manipulated. He spent a moment or so analysing the odds while the lads gripped themselves in anticipation of the verdict.

'OK.' Quiet as the approach of death. 'Just this once. But God help you all if you're not back at work Tuesday morning.'

'Yes, sir sir sir, thank sir sir, thank sir.' And they disappeared into cars and drove away before he could change his mind.

And they were late back. Come Tuesday morning,

'Where are they, Rob?' meaning bloody well find out or...

'Dunno sir.' But I had a good idea.

At 11o'clock I rang up the Coach House Inn in Bindura. The barman answered the phone and I asked him for anyone from Darwin.

'Wait one,' says he and shortly Jim came to the phone.

'If I were you, Jim,' says I, 'I'd get my arse back here quicker than greased light.'

'OK,' says he, but I knew it would be dark before we saw them.

At 7:30 pm I was sitting in the Changamire playing crib with Mike S.D.O. when we heard the approach of distant drums.

'I wonder,' says Mike, 'who that is.'

'I wonder.'

We weren't the only ones that heard them.

As they staggered into the Changamire, Doom was waiting with a message from Delta Charlie. He required the presence of his prodigal sons at 0700 hours next day in his Oscar Foxtrot Foxtrot India Charlie Echo.

And as they stood outside the boss's office the following morning our merry little band had undergone a transformation. They were, oh, like a pack of spent bloodhounds, the most unsavoury sight this side of a dustbin lid, a heap of remorseful refuse. They said you could hear the boss clearly, word for word, from the Police Camp. In my office it was loud enough and acrid enough to make the paintwork blush.

Shortly thereafter the trollops in head office discovered they were running out of D.C.s, the clever ones were getting the hell out while they could take cash and possessions with them and when they peered into the barrel's dark recesses who should they find lurking amidst the cabbage stalks and banana skins but me.

I remember one restless creature on the promotions board asking, 'How do you see the future of the ministry?' So I knew for a certainty his bags were packed.

And then they sent me to Kezi in Matabeleland, home of the fat Josh.

Before I had been there a week Jim rang to tell me Rob Dotito had been killed in an ambush and that his funeral would be the following Saturday at Gwelo.

When I got to Gwelo the lads were already arriving. We had arranged to stay at the same hotel and I remember Peter going up one elevator and coming back down the other two minutes later having lost his suitcase. We assembled in the lounge prior to leaving for the cemetery, and there everyone was introduced to Rob's father, a tall, powerful man I'd met years before elsewhere.

If there is anything cheap about death it is the reaction to it of those living, and at the funeral when people were falling apart all round him Rob's father stood silently at attention throughout the ceremony, like a great oak tree, before his son's grave. A tribute, paid with dignity and strength, worth more than all the tears.

And in the hotel that night the lads paid their own tributes, belting out 'Sweet Banana' on the drums, threatening the management with early retirement should they interfere, and getting thoroughly perforated. It's what you do at reunions. It's obligatory.

And if you listened carefully through the din you could hear Rob telling a story of how when Mac put up a building at Dotito and the D.C. said the roof wasn't level Mac replied,

'No sir. The roof's level. It's the floor that isn't level.'

CHAPTER 20

KEZI

My two years at Kezi I spent, like many another who believed himself the breakwater amidst tides of recent African history, organising elections, in the forlorn hope of finding a gram of honour among treacherous politicians, while knowing in my heart that I was suicidally pulling the plug out and washing my future down the drain. Elections we implemented with the energy of burning Christians, elections that, like a waiting epicentre, would drag us relentlessly, irresistibly down into the vortex and ultimate oblivion.

Elections. If there wasn't one brightly shining on the horizon and lighting up the landscape with promises of fresh, internationally acceptable, social and political oppression, we were sorting out the debris left by one that had scarce dimmed. And when new flags went up we took paint pots to our ogre spots and went about in skins of a trendier, more fashionable nature. Mass murderers we put on pedestals and revered as saints, saints we sent to prison. Life was one long joke.

Take the Muzorewa elections. Thatcher, as yet but a name on a ballot paper, sent us a delegation, an assorted crew possessing no ship, under the weary leadership of Viscount Boyd who believed himself still on duty in Nigeria, to satisfy no-one but herself that elections I came close to getting the sack for calling 'playing games' were free and fair. Yet as far as the blinkered tits we referred to as politicians were concerned, she bridged with hope the chasms of their waning resolve.

The elections themselves got the boot because, though initially sanctioned in principle by an anxious world, such approval fell away when Kaunda who, being king of a crumbling castle, shouted 'fix'. He had lumped his hopes of restoration on Nkomo, a waddling great no-hoper, who before the year was done would be lying on his political back like a stranded beetle. So, 'fix' they became and a year later we were at it again. Politicians.

So the Muzorewa elections, as they were known, were a debacle from the very outset but we resignedly went through the motions, peppering the district with polling stations, using schools, police camps, rest camps and whatever and, apart from an ambush during a deployment to the north, everything went smoothly enough. Halfway through the week however we were informed that Boyd and his cronies were flying in for a cuppa and look-see at the station in Kezi itself which we had housed in the courtroom.

So with haste and trepidation we cut down the peasants that hung by their necks, like scarecrows, from the ornamental trees that grew around the office, we uprooted the stocks and hid them temporarily in a store-room, and we even removed the ankle-irons worn as part of their uniform by African staff who prepared tea. We need not have hurried however because like all people who can trace their lineage back to the Virgin Mary, they were late and by the time their plane arrived the cakes and sandwiches were off playing somewhere. I remember hoping that Russell was their pilot but he wasn't.

'Perhaps,' I heard someone say, 'they've been shot down.'

'Another Viscount disaster,' from another.

It was a jolly little bunch of red-kneed pommie diplomats that stepped off the plane and my P.C., a rude, severe man who was with them, was clearly bored to the gills by their alert yet patronising company.

Proceedings in the courtroom, it was clear, they found tedious to the point of distraction, a fact Boyd scarce bothered to conceal as he shuffled unerringly exitwards, so that when we emerged into the sunlight he decided to fly the flag briefly and waylaid a couple of ragged peasants whose heads, now that they'd partaken of democracy's holy waters, were hell-bent in the direction of a beer-drink taking place a few yards down the road.

'Would you ask them,' says he favouring me with a weary smile, 'if they're happy with their vote? Would you mind?'

'How,' I translated, 'are the crops, gentlemen?' They picked their noses and looked skywards.

'Ayee. But we are crying, sir. There is no rain.'

'They say they're very happy,' says I.

'And are they happy with the organisation?'

'What about the cattle. Will they survive winter?'

'Ayee. But there are no sales. They will die,' they replied.

'Very happy.'

And putting the jolly interlude behind us, we headed eagerly for my office, the tea and the cakes. Spying loaded lemon trees, Boyd asked if he might have fresh lemon with his tea. When a lemon duly arrived, neatly sliced on a fresh plate, it seemed to enshrine man's blithering ways and the merry-go-round he has made of God's great gift.

I found myself cornered briefly by Boyd and after he'd made a few piddling enquiries into local political matters which, knowing he already had answers, I didn't deign to acknowledge, I asked what we could expect of Thatcher if she got her mitts on the reins of power.

Let me teach you a little game you can play next time you find yourself flumboozled by the mindless bleatings of a paid demagogue. It will enable you to see behind the words and into the underworld of intrigue they refer to as their minds. It's called 'Spot the rat'. I might market it. For instance -

'Never in a thousand years,' is rat-speak for – 'Tomorrow morning at half past six.'

'I shall never leave Rhodesia,' means – 'I have bought a farm in South Africa.'

'The whites have nothing to fear in an independent Zimbabwe,' is – 'I can't leave yet as I don't have enough cash in my overseas account.'

'I wish independent Zimbabwe a happy and successful future,' is - 'I hope the fucking place crumbles in weeks.' This is said dough-faced from the stoop of the new farmhouse in South Africa.

'Whites must stay and help Mr. Mugabe . . . ,' but the noise of jet engines drowns the rest.

Just remember they're gutless, that their spiritual fibre is held together by thoughts exclusively of self, and they won't mislead you.

So, when Boyd had finished spraying my face with semi-digested cake-bits, he looked down at his unpolished shoes, rolled his head from side to side, scratched his bum, coughed and said (watch that bum-scratching mannerism, by the way. It means the lie they're about to tell is so transparent even they can see through it),

'If Mrs. Thatcher forms the next government she will have no choice but to accept the results of the present elections as a true reflection of the political aspirations of the people of Zim, er, Rhodesia.'

Which was all I wanted to know.

On our way back to the plane a butterfly flew by, a common enough specimen.

'Oh look,' says Boyd. 'What a lovely butterfly. Does anyone know what it is?'

He didn't expect simple, trusting Rhodesians to know anything of course, he, on the other hand, being British, knowing everything.

'It's a swallow-tail,' says I. 'Commonly known as the orange dog. Its Greek name is Papilio Demodokos.'

My P.C., not missing a single lunge or parry in all this verbal sword-play, threw back his head and roared with laughter.

'Yes,' says Boyd, nonplussed. 'I used to breed them in Nigeria.' Meaning? Correct. He bred rabbits in Wales.

My staff, all eager to know, gathered round me as the plane flew over the cuckoo's nest.

'Be ready,' I told them, 'for more elections next year.'

And thus it is that, come February 1980, you can find us quietly flexing flabby administration muscles in the knowledge that during the next couple of months we will need to show ourselves capable of artistry, ingenuity, of changing chameleon-like the colour of bureaucratic tape from red to green, yellow, blue and purple so as to blend with ever-changing diplomatic and political backgrounds.

Don't get me wrong. Little managerial muscle is required to bang in ballot boxes. No great gifts are needed to change the faces that put up taxes and the price of petrol, to replace one lot of parliamentary idiots with another. Nothing could be simpler. We could have held elections weekly, as the Italians do, and still found time to play cricket and drink ourselves into oblivion. No, what gave us the heebie-jeebies, brought on the galloping willies, was that, this time, the British would be along to assist us.

The British, God help us.

For starters, every D.C. gets a supervisor, someone who is either a former colonial D.C. or an executive from local government in the U.K. He is there to spy while appearing to be asleep, to ensure fair play (I ask you. Fair play), and reassure Third World governments that wouldn't know a ballot box from a side-arm that we would get up to none of the tricks for which they are so laughably notorious.

Kezi was relatively fortunate - Kezi got Harry. The moment he stepped from the Land Rover it was clear Harry had few illusions. A former D.C. from Sierra Leone, cheerful, elegant and greying, he now lived in Bolton (from a king to a jack) where he administered a dogs' training home. I had no intention of beating around bushes. For his first day of work I had an extra chair brought to my office.

'My goodness no,' says he. 'I don't intend sitting here like a guard dog. You have work to do and I would only be a pest.'

But he had his orders from above and for the next six weeks we sat either side of the desk and gazed mindlessly at each other's ugly mugs.

For regular staff, elections formed but a drop in an administrative ocean, but attempts on my part to steer clear of the wretched things and keep the ship on a routine course were continually thwarted by Harry whose existence had been created by them. He pestered me interminably with questions about regulations, procedures, law, logistics, our different duties, background noises, and when he wasn't interrogating me he was briefing me. For his bosses in Bulawayo, terrified witless of criticism, both honest and imbecilic, from black African states, continually shifted the goal-posts and required endless meetings with their supervisors who, if no-one else, needed to know where to find them. They ha-ha had to be on the ball.

Everyone, meanwhile, ignored what was happening in the bush where the real elections were taking place - tribal people already had their orders on how to vote - and though we flirted outrageously with democracy we were married, mundanely as usual, to the demands of international expediency. True to modern political manoeuvring it was all a load of crap, but we played ball, Harry and I, he in his small corner and I in mine.

The phone would ring. 'For you, Harry.'

Five minutes later he'd look up, sigh. 'Guess what.'

'Changed again?'

'Changed again.'

But it was only a myriad times a day and all eternity yawned vacantly before us.

Unknown to us when he arrived, Harry had problems with his digestive tract, problems that from time to time – when for instance the local cook we had hired for him dished up goat's blood on toast and overdid the onions – he would gently complain of. He believed it to be ulcers and asked one day if he might go see the government doctor.

Doc was a refugee from Czechoslovakia who hadn't seen his family for seventeen years and letters allowed in and out by the Czech authorities were his only communication. He was a clever and capable man, a fact he disguised with rough and ready ways whenever patients were around.

The first time I went to see him he showed me brutally round his hospital, pleasure radiating from his pallid face as we zigzagged round trolleys and dirty bed linen that cluttered up the wards, as we squeezed ourselves into his slovenly operating theatre and gazed admiringly at the healthy state of his toilets.

During our tour of the wards a young African boy, who had been caught in cross-fire, complained that he threw up blood whenever he coughed. Doc paused at the side of the bed and gripped the boy's chin between powerful thumb and forefinger like a robot crushing an empty tin.

'Don't cough,' says Doc and we passed on to the next bed.

Doc's enthusiasm tried me and I hated visiting the hospital as a result. He always had a problem and was as restless as the sea until I sorted it out.

'Ah,' he would say the moment he saw me. 'Zere is somesink I wish you should see.' And it would be a problem.

Take your arm. It could be hanging from your shoulder by a millimetre of skin but Doc would brush past you, causing you to faint, with -

'Ah. Zere is somesink I wish you should see.'

And you went to see it knowing that for Doc treatment was temporarily not an issue.

He was a lonely man but rarely socialised with the whites in Kezi preferring as he did the company of young African belles who kept house for him. Perhaps it's a Czech custom – I must check it out one day – but he would come into the local store where others of us were having a cold beer and buy underwear for these awesome, brown maidens. He would select, say, a pair of black knickers, hold them aloft and say -

'Yes?'

while the girl shook her sullen head at him and looked down her nose.

Then, in a ritual as mundane as it was intimate, Doc would hold up another pair, then another, then another. When at last the girl saw knickers she liked she would nod her head and Doc would go on to bras.

I imagined him in his house at night listening reverently to Mozart with a bevy of these beauties lolling uncomprehendingly about the room like mahogany figurines in the underwear of their choice.

So I took Harry to see him.

'Ah. Zere is somesink I wish you should see.' And it was, of course, a problem.

When I had seen and attended to it, Doc handed Harry a bottle of vitamin C tablets and a gallon of muck that masqueraded as medicine. Harry's problem wasn't ulcers.

'Zat man is not well.' Doc confided as we left, and Doc was right.

Two months after he returned to Bolton the doctors opened Harry up and discovered not ulcers but cancer, incurably advanced, and ten days later he was gone.

Shortly before the elections were due I walked into my office and found Chief Mathe sitting quietly in an easy chair. I had known him years before when I was stationed in an adjacent district.

'To what do I owe . . . ?' I began.

You had to know Mathe; a towering figure of fearsome aspect, with many wives and children, he had little time for small talk.

'I wish to invite you to my kraal,' says he. 'Will Saturday do?'

And, being badly in need of a break from vaudeville, I replied,

'Erm, Saturday. Well, yes, OK.'

'Early evening then.'

'Why now, Chief,' I asked, 'of all times?'

'You used to visit me regularly,' he said. 'But this will be the last time.' He paused. 'The new government will not allow it.' Mathe, being an Ndebele, was thinking, of course, of the jealous ways of Mugabe and his Shona people.

And he left before I could stop him.

'You will stay at my kraal tonight,' said Chief Mathe,

'Thank you very much, Chief,' says I. It was late summer and my work as a District Commissioner frequently took me to the bush where I had been treated with quite extraordinary hospitality, particularly by chiefs, so that the early evening found me standing apprehensively outside the fence that surrounded the kraal while I waited for an invitation to enter. I was relieved therefore when the chief appeared from one of the huts.

'Ngena,' he called. 'Come in.' And when I had made my way inside, we sat silently in the lengthening shadow of a tall mahogany tree while a crimson sun, sinking fast, threw purple shafts of colour across a dying sky. A sudden flurry of activity briefly occupied my attention as a host of chickens, squawking furiously, fled past, closely pursued by a young man bearing a large knife. The confusion was lovely if short-lived, and when the boy reappeared he bore in one hand a large cockerel, headless and dripping, which he held up for his father's approval.

'Kulungile,' (O.K.) said his father, before turning to me. 'Do you like Zimbabwe?' he asked.

'Very . . . ,' but I was brought to a halt by a young girl who smilingly placed at our feet a large bowl of African beer. 'My daughter,' he said with no apparent emotion. He raised the bowl to his lips, took a good slug, rubbed his mouth with the palm of his hand and passed it on.

'My wives are preparing umumbu,' he announced as if excusing their absence. (Umumbu is made, usually, by boiling crushed maize in water and stirring it until it is the consistency of thick porridge.)

146

Time passed unnoticed and as the encroaching shadows deepened, and darkness overtook the kraal, busy people were seen flickeringly in darting firelight, or sitting ghost-like in the fierce white light of fizzing lamps.

The beer, I was alarmed to note, was beginning to take a serious hold and I was grateful when the chief said, 'Come,' and led me inside a nearby hut. There stood before us a small table and two large mugs and we were immediately joined by more daughters bearing, inevitably, more beer, umumbu, roast chicken and a bowl of spinach containing crushed groundnuts. When the girls had left us we laid into the glorious spread before us, rolling the umumbu into little balls and dipping it into everything. The chief began pouring yet more beer and as he did so the family gathered outside and the strains of melancholy African music drifted in on the air, matching my melancholy mood.

At the end of it all, we washed our hands in a bowl of warm water and retired to yet another hut that contained a bed and two chairs. As the mugs were being filled, Mathe told me how, years before, he had visited England and met Queen Elizabeth. He pointed at the walls where I saw for the first time pictures of Her Majesty and her father, George VI.

'Stand,' said the chief.

We stood respectfully to attention before the pictures of the Royal Graces, and then, as the national anthem came to an end I said to Mathe,

'If you will forgive me, Chief, I really must retire. I have much to do tomorrow.'

'Very well, sir,' says he. 'I will send my oldest daughter.'

I made it to the bed, virgo intacta, and the next thing I knew, the sun was pouring through the half-open door, and next to my bed a small, square table had appeared, and on it a cup of warm tea, biscuits and a couple of chicken sandwiches.

CHAPTER 21

A VACANT CHIEFTAINSHIP

Before the elections arrived to drive everybody up the wall, out of the air-vents and down the road to the local funny farm, I had been involved, and still was, in another election, that of a replacement for a vacant chieftainship.

It went thus.

Gorya Khumalo was in his late twenties when this important chieftainship became vacant. He was the only surviving male descendant of Sidotshiwe Khumalo, son of Lobengula Khumalo, who, like his father Mzilikazi before him, was king of the Ndebele Nation, and therefore the only legitimate candidate for the vacant post. Like his famous forebears, he was an immense man, by far the biggest man I had ever known, and if you stood anywhere near him he obliterated the sun. Like Lennie in *Of Mice and Men* he was gentle and kind, but, unlike Lennie, he was well aware of his strength.

Sometimes I would look at him when his mind was elsewhere, and have visions of him plucking light aircraft out of the sky and eating the pilot and passengers, but of course he would never do such a thing, he being gentle 'n' all, but I warned pilots using the Kezi airstrip just in case. He was like the elephant whose trunk is so powerful it can lift a thousand-pound log, yet so sensitive it can pick up a needle.

Gorya was a beer-hall policeman, employed by the local African council to whom the beer-hall belonged. The council made a great deal of money from its beer-halls so long as the council secretary didn't get to it first, and it provided capital for building schools, clinics whatever, and the maintenance of roads and water supplies. Gorya was paid a pittance.

Now the beer-hall was a focal point of social activity and the locals would meet there to drink, smoke, gossip, place bets, flirt, punch each other up, and it was the latter activity for which Goriya was essentially employed. He also guaranteed the safety of the beer-hall, the hooligan element having more sense than to try Gorya's formidable patience. Even terrorists who regularly raided other beer-halls - a guaranteed source of funds, intoxication and, with luck, sex; in a word, Paradise - gave Gorya's a wide berth. He was, like other Zulus, fearless.

He monthly saved the council thousands because his presence made of the beer-hall the safest meeting place in a hundred-mile radius, and yet he received poverty-line wages. He was blessed with humility to add to his other virtues and would never complain, so I decided it was time for me to go see flog, erm, Chairman of Council.

'Would council be prepared to pay Gorya more money?' I asked.

'The council has no money,' he replied.

'It would have no money,' saith I, 'but for Gorya.'

It was common enough knowledge that tribespeople never paid their taxes and that council did nothing to recover such debts. Councillors, much like their counterparts worldwide, were never seen in public once they had been elected, so that ordinary people had no idea what council was doing for them. Which, I add hastily, was usually nothing. Because it had no money, because. . .

The council's sole source of income was therefore the beer-hall, and my next shaft hit the bull's eye.

'If council doesn't pay Gorya another forty dollars a month, (twice what he presently earned) I will find him employment in the D.C.'s offices.'

End of story, beginning of song.

I asked Gorya what he would do if he were elected chief.

'I would try to help,' was his simple, devastating reply.

He had, however, a rival claimant to the throne.

Now, in order to have any claim to the chieftainship, you would have to be, ideally, the oldest surviving son, failing which a close relative (Gorya was Sidotshiwe's grandson), a distant relative which might lead to war as it had done with Lobengula before a conclusion was reached, and failing all else at least a member of the Ndebele Tribe, but things should never really get that far. They did, but they shouldn't.

Gorya's rival, if my memory serves me right, was none of the above, being (memory, please) a member of the Kalanga Tribe, and he rarely visited Matabeleland, and only then when he was on the make. The fact that he had rustled up enough support simply to enter the race was due in most part that, over no little time, he had bribed, bought and begged his way into the good graces of a loud but influential minority of people, mainly businessmen and professionals, who would look the other way when the truth of the matter emerged.

Life is easy once you get the hang of it, and I was onto this fellow in a flash. To be honest, I did have a head start.

Disturbing my afternoon's kip one day, my sergeant came into the office and announced,

'Senator M....... to see you, sir.'

See. Senator. Piece of cake.

'Thank you, Sergeant. Please show him in.'

A tall, thin, smooth fellow he was, but with restless eyes that straightway took in the office, the simple furnishings, the array of phones (I could have been running a betting shop), the safe, the map of the district, and the F.N. rifle in the corner. He started at the rifle, and that interested me.

'Does the rifle disturb you, Senator?' I asked. 'I can have it removed.'

'No, no, no, no, no. It was just unexpected.'

There was a war on just round the corner. Unexpected?

He was beautifully turned out - a good suit, elegant shoes, a club-of-some-sort tie. He had come, of course, to get a good look at me and, after the pleasantries, he left. My sergeant, a good man to have on your side, hated him, knowing him to be an imposter.

The next time I saw the senator, I asked, as I had Gorya - only more out of amusement than anything else:

'What would you do if you were elected chief?' And people say I have no sense of humour.

I, not as yet being aware of his sinister, senatorial cunning, underestimated him, believing he had no chance in the face of Gorya's impeccable credentials.

He clapped his hand on his chest, took a deep breath and, like a candidate for the American Presidency, held forth something thus:

'If the good people of Matabeleland elect me chief, I will first and foremost make sure that every family has enough food to eat, there will be work for everyone, I will build schools so that every child has access to an education, I will build clinics to provide good health services, every kraal will receive piped water, electricity will be made available to all regardless . . . '

I tried to stop him, politely, before he began colonising neighbouring countries.

'I will eliminate racism, ageism, feminism, fanaticism ... '

'Yes, yes, yes. Thank you.'

He was back in the senate, of course, having forgotten, in his reverie, where he was. God. How do we put up with them?

This devious little bastard - I will call him Noddy - believed himself to be above the law or, more likely, that the law could be persuaded to take a brief break in the Bahamas, thus 'leaving him the world to bustle in' (Richard III, another devious little bastard), or most likely of all that the law had not yet arrived in isolated tribal areas like Kezi.

He was to discover, however, that the law had long tentacles, and that these tentacles had not only found their way into isolated tribal areas, but insinuated themselves into every nook, cranny and crevice that contained life.

About half a mile north of Kezi village a large cattle kraal had been built, and in it were housed some 200 cattle. These beasts were the offspring of Lobengula's original herd and were the property of the house of Khumalo. So, whoever acceded to the throne would inherit them. Their value at a D.C.'s cattle sale, they being well looked after and in prime condition, would be in the region of 20,000 dollars.

You'll never guess what happens next.

Noddy came to me one day with the news that he intended to drive these cattle to his home. I had no idea where 'home' was, but no matter. He was unashamedly, openly announcing himself legal heir to the chieftainship, and that the cattle were therefore his. In case anyone doubted his intentions, he had trucks and drivers standing by, ready to load up and drive away.

My sergeant was rigid with anger.

I made it quite clear to Noddy that if he removed so much as the bristles that sprouted from their foreheads, he would find himself a guest for the night in one of his government's cells.

He nodded knowingly and left. But I knew from the look in his eyes that the gauntlet had been accepted, and that he would be back.

A few days afterwards, my sergeant burst in with the news that Noddy was loading up Lobengula's cattle prior to carting them away.

I phoned my friend who was member-in-charge, Police. We had discussed the matter at length, and half an hour later Noddy found himself behind bars, charged with theft.

His lawyer took no time calling me from Salisbury - he seemed to have expected the news - and getting no change from the glowing picture he painted of the man, he tried muscle.

'The senator is no man of straw, you know.'

'I don't care if he's the prime minister,' I replied.

There was laughter from the other end, and I saw no more of Noddy 'til the day of the 'big meeting' at which the chieftainship would be decided. It was, however, time (overdue, to be honest) for me to do some research.

My predecessor, a good and decent man, had left a pile of paperwork behind him, detailing the strength of Noddy's claim to the chieftainship and strangely, I thought, Gorya's less convincing claim. I didn't believe, however, that he had done much research, relying more on word of mouth, mainly Noddy's, the mouth, that is, of a politician, and at the 'big meeting' I knew which mouth would have 'the ayes'.

I hastened to Bulawayo, and spent, in all, a couple of days in the city museum, looking at faded photos, ancient documents detailing tribal movements, allegiances, family trees, second-class dissertations in strangled English, and strange letters. There were reams of stuff regarding the Khumalos, and even bits on fringe characters such as Cecil Rhodes, and when I thought I had all the evidence I needed, my way forward seemed clear. I had been able to confirm much of what I had been told by tribal elders - chiefs, headmen and kraalheads, a couple of them in their nineties and able therefore to speak from memory, though this source of information had to be used with caution.

Elders were generally reliable in terms of accuracy, though the more advanced in years needed to be handled with care. They were fragile and might fall asleep mid-sentence, or they would wander down other lanes of their memory and have to be dragged back to the matter in hand, and never arrange an interview for the afternoon because they might spend their lunch at the beer-hall, or beer drinks closer to home, and would be useless to you for the rest of the day. They might speak in a barely-audible harsh whisper, in which case the hordes of small children that invariably gathered round these affairs would come in handy. On the whole, however, all went well. And whatever their afflictions, none of them were stupid, and I felt myself able to believe the stories stowed away in their memories.

I scarce recognised my sergeant in his Sunday best, and when he knocked on my door I had to get my bearings. The Khumalo family were waiting to see me at the office.

I told him it was out of the question as I had a severe attack of gout and could barely walk. The office was a mere two hundred yards away but if you have suffered from gout . . .

'O.K.' says he. 'I will get you a walking stick,' and disappeared. He was back twenty minutes later with a stick from the hospital, but things were not good.

There were a dozen or so members of the family waiting for me outside the office, all male, all in their twenties to forties, a young and vigorous bunch and not the ancients I had expected. Once inside the office I was asked about the limp and, when I explained gout, one of them informed me that Lobengula suffered from gout and that some of the family had inherited it. Which broke the ice. They then asked the question they had come to ask: how had my visit to Bulawayo gone?

I couldn't in fact discuss it, but I could tell them not to worry and did so. They were quiet and serious and clearly wanted to know more. The silence was broken by,

'So we needn't worry, sir?' says a young man at the back.

'No,' I said.

His elders and betters gave the youngster a good ballocking for his nerve, but there was no anger. They then suggested I meet Violet

- a meaningful look at sergeant, who would have to act as go-between
- and left.

Like all the Khumalos, Violet was a big person. She lived at Entumbane in the Matopos Hills, north of Kezi, where she was guardian of Lobengula's shrine, i.e. she saw to the upkeep of the place. I knew that Mzilikazi and Sidotshiwe were buried there but not Lobengula. She explained that when he died in South Africa his remains had been brought back in his wagon and settled in Emtumbane with the others. The spirits of deceased Ndebele chiefs spoke through the female of the line and Violet was the present incumbent. Lobengula's spirit made a nuisance of itself as we shall see.

I had been to Entumbane where I had lunch with her and I was ashamed to find that an iron fence had been erected round the entrance - the shrine sat in a shallow cave - because Lobengula's wagon had been cannibalised by foreign tourists, and though the wheels were still there, there was little else. I also learned that tourists had stolen many of Lobengula's personal belongings, historically valuable objects, his dagger included.

The dagger sticks in my memory because the first time Violet invaded my office she was wearing a replica of it about her waist, which made her look quite formidable. She darted and swirled about, picking up everything that wasn't nailed down, studying carefully everything that was, and I got a blurred image of silks, animal furs, finger rings, earrings and bracelets, beads, bones and buttons.

Her messages from Lobengula were always dominated by his desire to see a secondary school built in the Matopos area. Canny fellow, Lobengula, for there wasn't a secondary school outside Bulawayo and it was keenly needed.

During the latter half of my time in Kezi, I battled unsuccessfully with various authorities, local, provincial and national, in an attempt to get things moving. I submitted, oh God, reports that no one ever read and visited offices that I found occupied by a new generation, young, ambitious people who didn't know how things worked and didn't want to. They were the 'upwardly mobile' generation. If they had worked for me, they would certainly have been upwardly mobile - helped on their way by my right boot. In a few offices I found people I knew, old hands who were hanging on for their pensions and were fearful of involvement lest they lose these rights. They all did, anyway, eventually.

The infrastructure for getting things done was there but it had fallen apart. Thousands of bureaucrats were employed at huge sums of money to record and document vast plans for development, but they committed them to files which in turn found their way into filing cabinets where nobody ever disturbed them again. Bit like the United Nations, come to think about it.

I got nowhere and I would doubt if, to this day, Lobengula got his secondary school. He was a generation too late.

Come the great day, the day when the new chief would be elected. The meeting would take place in the D.C.'s courtroom, and I watched from my office window as officials in their capacities of things I'd never heard of began to arrive. Among them the P.C. and my predecessor standing in a huddle with Noddy. And to make matters really bad, the Khumalo family had been left outside. A small breeze of apprehension brushed against my cheeks.

'Ah, to hell with it,' I thought and got on with administrative demands.

At around 6 o'clock, having been cloistered together for well on five hours, they emerged. My P.C. sought me out.

'They've chosen Noddy, I'm afraid,' he said.

We both knew what had happened.

The Khumalos, also knowing what had happened, popped their heads into my office and acknowledged the fact that I had done all I could.

Ordinary tribal people, whatever their rank, are easily manipulated by politicians who, once in a life-time, descend from Olympus and allow themselves to be seen - and, of course, heard. Proud, if simple, they may be, but faced with officious, headquarters authority, they can be transformed, becoming servile, robotic, almost mindless.

Not always, of course. And not everyone. Which was why Noddy had had the Khumalo family kept outside. They would have torn his throat out.

'Ah well,' I said to the P.C. 'They may not know it, or maybe they do, but their problems have only just started.'

I heard later, after I had left Kezi, that Noddy had opened a string of illegal shops, including a butcher's. Now where, I wondered, did he get the meat?

The elections, meanwhile, steamed ahead but they needed continually to negotiate British icebergs.

I don't know why this is written so large and indelibly on my memory but I walked one day into my office and found Harry riffling through a book behind my desk. I crept up beside him.

'Anything you fancy?' says I.

'Oh,' says he, looking silly. 'There you are.' He replaced the book he had removed – a copy of Herodotus' Histories – and sat down.

I doubt anyone under the age of forty, education having given way to the fart-arsed, meddling doctrines of equality, will know who Herodotus was, but as I sat and gazed at Harry's ugly mug I found myself wondering what the reaction of Herodotus and his fellow ancients would have been to the shameless gang-rape now being perpetrated by the spiteful, lustful world upon the honour of a proud if simple nation. Spiritual desolation, no doubt, followed by draughts of hemlock.

Then there were the – let the timpanists blow their tympana – British Provincial Supervisors. These super-drips went round D.C. stations monitoring the way things were proceeding. Monitoring like the treacherous lizards they were, watching, waiting, while Rhodesia was thrown to the crocs. When we first met we were mutually suspicious, they of me because the D.C. at another station, a student of British history, had treated them with unveiled contempt, meeting irresistible mandate with immovable non-compliance.

And I of them because, well, nature has a way. The world is full of people with a nature of some sort or another.

They patted everything that moved merrily on the back. Checked the ham sandwiches for bugs – mechanical and invertebrate – whispered incessantly in dark corners with the supervisor, and created problems to give it all meaning and make life look authentic.

After about ten minutes it dawned on me that one of them, Dick, yes, Dick, who I thought had been wandering harmlessly through a maze of diplomatic small-talk, was trying to tell me *summut*. As he gabbled on about how to make omelettes without breaking eggs it became clear slowly that what he was really saying was that it might just possibly be a good plan, frying pan, did I not feel, eggs with peel, given time to organise and assuming logistics would allow, simple when you know how, if only to please, tomato or cheese, we...

'You'd like a mobile then,' says I, tiring rapidly.

'Well now. That might be an idea.' He nodded enthusiastically while Harry and I made unseen sigh contact.

A mobile station was a polling station that went on wheels to the people instead of the idle bastards to it. We had nine stations already that more than adequately covered the district but what Dick wanted was a bit of a show. And the reason he was pooing everywhere was that Kezi was the home of Joshua Nkomo and he feared criticism from the fat slob if he didn't have a mobile. Everybody else had one...

So I said OK. You can have a mobile but in exchange I want a Union Jack for my son. God, we were devil-may-care in those days. I got the flag and when I'd inspected it for traps Dick got his mobile.

A few days before the elections were due, Harry was called to Bulawayo for one of his meetings and I arranged to collect him and the election paraphernalia the day after. I met him at the P.C.'s office. Says he to me, 'You'll never guess.'

'Changed again.'

'The fools,' says he, feigning high blood-pressure. 'The bloody fools. They have decided to bring British policemen out, one for each polling station.'

Well, I knew what was behind that. People who cannot be trusted themselves – black states, brown states, white, yellow, green and blue states – cannot trust others.

'Good,' says I.

'Ye gads. I thought you'd blow apart.'

'Why should I. The more the merrier. The whole thing's a bloody comedy anyway. Let's get your British M.P.s out here as well and make a Broadway Production of it.'

We then collected all our election equipment, signed for it in centuplicate, and returned to Kezi.

The Brit Bobs – when you need one you can't find one anywhere – didn't arrive as it happened until lunch-time the day prior to the launching and we had to keep the trucks, equipment, election personnel, and assorted camp-followers waiting 'til the absolutely last moment. So when they finally appeared I told them which stations would be their ha-ha homes for the next seven days, whisked them off to the club for a lightning-fast beer, and at 2 o'clock *exactement* everyone set off, Bob helmets, so familiar the world over, bobbing incongruously against a background of raw African bush and out of jolly old sight.

I heaved a sigh of relief.

When Harry and I visited stations during the week, the Brits confided themselves shocked by the facts of African life.

'Back home,' they would say, 'they have no idea. No idea at all. We've all been brainwashed.' Amen.

It had been hammered into them, for instance, that only the blind and crippled should be assisted in casting their vote, but they discovered, to their innocent wonder, that one in four people, healthy and otherwise, required careful guidance, advice and tuition as to where he/she should make his/her mark. Because simple peasants didn't know, despite months of ZAPU instruction in ubiquitous bush classes, which column was Joshua, or, when this had been explained, where exactly they should put their cross.

So, it being much quicker and easier, the Bobs made the mark for them and in this way had a telling influence on events in Rhodesia. They'd still be there now had they been faithful to their mandates and Mugabe should be sending them cigars at Christmas with little 'Thank you' notes. After all, they put him in.

On one of my rounds I bumped into Sir Carlisle Burton, and that evening before he left we had a few drinks and a chat in the club. I asked him if he could get me a job in the West Indies.

'Oh why?' says he.

'Do I really need to explain?'

'So you see these elections as the end of your career in Rhodesia.'

'Career? Everything.' We must have been mad.

'And how long do you think you have?'

'Ten minutes.'

He gave me his card and said to keep in touch. He was a philatelist and though I sent him Rhodesian stamps he said he needed, he never returned the compliment. You can trust no-one anymore.

When Mugabe's victory had been announced, the P.C. invited D.C.s, staff and families to a hotel in Bulawayo and as we arrived we found the British Supervisors sitting in the lounge. I went up to them and spoke.

'Well, I suppose you're all buggering off to your smug little homes in the U.K. with your double glazing, wall-to-wall carpeting, central heating, colour T.V., pension fund and national health service now that you and the South Africans have fucked everything up here.'

But all I got was averted eyes and silence which was a pity. I was in the mood for a slanging match.

Harry and I said our farewells and two months later he was gone forever.

I was tired now of playing comedy parts but, like it or not, one small farcical encore remained. I went to my A.D.C. and spoke.

'Look, I'm off into the bush for some fresh air. Independence Day is next Saturday. Just organise the bloody thing and I'll walk on and make the speeches.'

And a right good show he made of it. There were beer tents, food for the masses, football matches – it was like a day at the fair – and standing in the background, lest we forget the noisome mission, seats and a flag-pole. I nearly said scaffold. As the masses began to gather I went to pick up visiting dignitaries (Latin 'dignus', 'worthy') from the airfield in a Mercedes we'd borrowed from an oppressed African mass. I gave them all a couple of drinks in the club, and as I drove them up to the fairground I felt like the leader of a lynching party looking for a rope.

I made the speech from the throne amid peasant jeering, a dignitary (where the hell do we get these words) replied on behalf of the British P.M. amid peasant silence, the old flag came down amid peasant confusion, the new one went up amid peasant indifference, and we were about to retire to the beer tent amid peasant relief when Steven Nkomo, brother of Josh, rocked up - rats.

He staggered to the microphone amid peasant hysteria and made a rambling speech in Sindebele, the local language. He set the tone and no mistake for a brave, new, reconciliatory Zimbabwe.

'Do not worry,' he told the gathering, 'that we have a Shona government. It will not be for long. The Ndebele nation will rise again and the Shona dogs will hunt for us.' This sent them all crazy.

Steven offered me a job in administration with his brother's party but I was tired of being on the losing side and told him to stick it.

I might have been mad. But I wasn't <u>that</u> mad.

Epilogue

The Impossible Dream

I told Harry a little story before he left.

It is just about a century since the first Native Commissioner trundled up to Mt. Darwin and built his first offices of mud and thatch. And today the club has no cocktail bar, no windows, no doors. The squash courts have become kitchens, the cooking taking place over open fires. The floor of the club hall is covered with the possessions of squatters, goat dung, chicken shit, and fireplaces. The tennis courts are distinguishable from the bush only by the fences that once surrounded them. The swimming pool is filled with bicycles, firewood, beer bottles, boxes, mattresses and leaves.

When Kissinger was going around trying to ditch us, we were told we would all get a handsome handshake payable outside Rhodesia. One night in the Changamire we were all discussing what we would do with the lolly.

We agreed that we would pool it and buy a small island in the Seychelles. We would rear cattle and sheep, grow vegetables and wheat, build a small hotel and brothel, raise the green and white flag. There would be no politicians, no journalists, and we would live out the rest of our lives in peace and serenity. We were much taken with the idea and there was great back-slapping until Jim says,

'Yes, and you know what? As soon as we've set up our little paradise and raised the flag some bastard will come along and take it off us.'

That took the wind out of our sails and we all went outside and played darts.

Which tickled old Harry.

ABOUT THE AUTHOR

Born in Redditch, Worcestershire, and educated at Redditch County High School and Cambridge University, Robin Walker emigrated with his young family to Rhodesia in the early sixties. Having taught English and Latin for some eight years, he joined the Ministry of Internal Affairs (Intaf) as a cadet District Officer, and became a District Commissioner five years later. He retired from the Ministry in November, 1980, by which time Rhodesia had become Zimbabwe. He and his wife finally left Zimbabwe in 1990 for Greece where for a while he taught English and then worked for a publishing company in Athens until his retirement. He now lives with his wife on a Greek island.

21855259R00088

Made in the USA
Charleston, SC
04 September 2013